£1.50.

CW00548021

LANGUAGE TURNED ON ITSELF

Language Turned On Itself

The Semantics and Pragmatics
of Metalinguistic Discourse

HERMAN CAPPELEN AND ERNIE LEPORE

OXFORD
UNIVERSITY PRESS

OXFORD

UNIVERSITY PRESS

Great Clarendon Street, Oxford OX2 6DP

Oxford University Press is a department of the University of Oxford.
It furthers the University's objective of excellence in research, scholarship,
and education by publishing worldwide in

Oxford New York

Auckland Cape Town Dar es Salaam Hong Kong Karachi
Kuala Lumpur Madrid Melbourne Mexico City Nairobi
New Delhi Shanghai Taipei Toronto

With offices in

Argentina Austria Brazil Chile Czech Republic France Greece
Guatemala Hungary Italy Japan Poland Portugal Singapore
South Korea Switzerland Thailand Turkey Ukraine Vietnam

Oxford is a registered trade mark of Oxford University Press
in the UK and in certain other countries

Published in the United States
by Oxford University Press Inc., New York

© Herman Cappelen and Ernie Lepore 2007

British Library Cataloguing in Publication Data
Data available

Library of Congress Cataloging in Publication Data
Data available

Typeset by Laserwords Private Limited, Chennai, India
Printed in Great Britain
on acid-free paper by
Biddles Ltd., King's Lynn, Norfolk

ISBN 978–0–19–923119–5

1 3 5 7 9 10 8 6 4 2

Ernie would like to dedicate this book to David C. Klein, Esq., whom he unofficially adopted as a parent twenty-five years ago. The relationship has worked out splendidly for him, and he hopes for David as well.

Herman would like to dedicate this book, with love and gratitude, to his mother, Kari

Preface

This book is about what happens when language turns on itself, when it becomes self-reflective. Those of us who think, talk, and write about language are compulsive consumers of various metalinguistic devices, but reliance on these devices begins early. Kids are told, 'That's called a 'rabbit' ' or 'She is not called 'spunipta', she's called 'Anita' '. It's not implausible that a primitive capacity for the metalinguistic kicks in at the inaugural stages of language acquisition. But no matter when or how frequently these devices are invoked, one thing is clear: they present theorists of language with a complex data pattern. We hope, at a minimum, to convince you that the study of these devices and patterns is not only interesting, but also carries important consequences for other parts of philosophy.

The history of the topic dates back at least to the origins of analytic philosophy. We find nascent theories of quotation in Frege and Wittgenstein. It is touched upon in various ways by other leading figures such as Tarski, Gödel, Carnap, Church, Reichenbach, and Quine. It is not, however, much of an exaggeration to say it became a serious topic of investigation only after Davidson's classic paper on quotation was published in 1979. Much of our earlier work on this topic is devoted to defending a version of Davidson's view. We have, however, become convinced that our earlier neo-Davidsonean position is fundamentally mistaken; so from a personal perspective this book represents a dramatic intellectual development: it is a systematic attempt to demolish positions held by our earlier time-slices. But those time-slices are not our only targets. The entire current literature on these topics is misguided. In the last two chapters of this book, we present a novel theory—this time with more humility and considerably more reservations than in our earlier attempts.

Our primary goal is not, however, to push one theory over another on our readers. Most of all we find the data fascinating and think of this book as an introduction to the subject matter for the uninitiated. It is important to array the data without the 'noise' of theory; hence the structure of the book. In Part I, before any theories are even mentioned, five chapters are devoted solely to presenting data about various aspects of our metalinguistic practices. Since there is such a high level of complexity at the data level and any interpretation of that data will depend on prior theoretical commitments (about semantics, pragmatics, and syntax), we doubt that there is one uniquely correct way to put it all into a coherent theory. In Part II, we turn to theory, first exposition and then criticism. And in the final two chapters we present our current effort to weave an adequate account of quotation wherever it occurs, though even this story we consider a work in progress.

Acknowledgments

This book was a long time in the writing (though perhaps not long enough). During that period, Lepore taught earlier drafts of the book first in a graduate seminar at Rutgers in the fall of 2004 and then in the spring of 2005 at the University of Santigao. He would like to thank the participants in both seminars for their input, especially Jerry Fodor, Jason Stanley, Adam Sennett, Michael Johnson and Eliza Block. Cappelen, against all sane professional advice, wrote his PhD dissertation, 'The Semantics of Quotation and the Metaphysics of Signs', on these topics more than ten years ago. Many of the central themes and theses from that work shaped his thinking about the topics of this book. His dissertation advisors, Stephen Neale, Charles Chihara, and John Searle, were important inflences on that initial work. Cappelen and Lepore together and separately and in collaboration with others wrote a string of papers during the ten plus years, zigzagging their way across the various positions discussed and criticized in the first ten chapters of this book, leading up to the semantic treatment and metaphysical position of the last two chapters. We both would like to thank Mario Torrente-Gomez, Ray Elugardo, and Paul Pietroski for reading an earlier draft of the manuscript for OUP and for providing us with terrific feedback, though we surely won't have adequately responded to all their helpful and insightful comments. Various drafts of various chapters were given at different department colloquia and conferences during the last few years (including the University of Kansas, the University of Toronto, the University of Oslo, the University of British Columbia, Vassar College, Simon Fraser University, the University of Florida, University College Dublin), and we would like to thank the audiences of these various sessions. Particularly useful was a conference on quotation held in Oslo in the fall of 2005. Special thanks go to Dan Blair, Josh Dever, Kirk Ludwig, Greg Ray, Francois Recanati, Marga Reimer, Mark Richard, Paul Saka, and Rob Stainton. Two individuals, however, merit extra-special kudos for numerous discussions on the topics of this book: Sam Cumming and John Hawthorne. Finally, we want to thank Federico Luzzi for his proofreading, Chiara Tabet for the index and both Peter Momtchiloff and Catherine Berry from OUP for their guidance throughout. We also gratefully acknowledge financial support for finishing this work from the Centre for the Study of Mind in Nature, at the University of Oslo.

Contents

1

Advertisement

To whatever extent it makes sense to compare the philosophical significance of various topics (and a strong case can be made that it doesn't; so take what follows with a grain of salt) quotation ought to have received more attention than, say, anaphora and quantifier domain restriction. Since these claims no doubt will strike non-aficionados as ludicrous, we begin by outlining some reasons for the practice of quotation being of central significance to the philosophy of language and to philosophy more generally. Our goal is to elicit a wide range of support for why quotation is an important but wrongly neglected philosophical topic. Treat what follows as an advertisement for theorizing about metalinguistic discourse—why the topic of quotation merits more consideration than it has received over the last century or so.

1.1. PRO-QUOTATION CAMPAIGN: SEVEN STEPS

In what follows we'll sketch seven topics that can be illuminated significantly by understanding quotation—together they constitute a strong *prima facie* case for its philosophical significance.

(a) Understanding Metalinguistic Discourse

When language is used to attribute properties to language or otherwise theorize about it, a device is needed that—to borrow Donald Davidson's apt phrase—'turns language on itself.' Quotation, by virtue of being our primary metalinguistic tool, is one such central device. If you don't understand it, you cannot understand (1.1)–(1.4):

1.1. 'Snow is white' is true in English iff snow is white.[1]
1.2. 'Aristotle' refers to Aristotle.

---

[1] We are restricting our quotation practice to using single quotes not because we are Anglophiles but for reasons of economy.

    1.3. 'The' is the definite article in English.
    1.4. 'Bachelor' has eight letters.

Nor do you fully understand what you are saying in claiming that
(1.1)–(1.4) are true. You don't understand what those claims *mean*
and you don't understand their *truth conditions*. That's an embarrassing
position to find yourself in if your business is theorizing about language;
especially since a number of philosophers have said in print that
sentences like (1.1) are true as a matter of meaning alone, that they
are analytically true. For example, according to the redundancy and
disquotational theories of truth (Ramsey 1927; Quine 1970), asserting
that a sentence is true is equivalent to asserting the sentence itself.
Asserting " 'Snow is white' is true" is equivalent to asserting 'Snow is
white'. If this is a synonymy claim, then we have every right to expect
these theorists to tell us which semantics for quotation underwrites their
claims. As a matter of fact, most extant theories of quotation do not.

    To illustrate our point, consider six influential theories about the
subject terms in (1.1)–(1.4): quotation expressions are:

    a. demonstratives demonstrating a pattern (Davidson),
    b. quantifiers ranging over tokens (a prior time-slice of Cappelen
       and Lepore),
    c. unstructured proper names referring to classes (Tarski),
    d. descriptions of concatenations of classes (Geach),
    e. functions referring to abstract entities (Richard), or
    f. illustrations (Recanati).

Each of (a)–(f) has implications for the meanings and truth conditions
of (1.1)–(1.4)—incompatible implications; (a)–(f) attribute radically
different (interpretive) truth conditions and propositions to (1.1)–(1.4).
Not all these theories will, for example, validate the analyticity of (1.1).

    Theories of quotation concern not just *logical form* but also *semantic
value*. One central issue in the literature is what each grammatical subject
in (1.1)–(1.4) is quoting. Is it a set, a property, or some other kind of
abstract object? Is it a token? Is it the kind of historically stretched-out
object Kaplan calls a 'common currency word' (Kaplan 1990: 95)? Can
it quote any one of these; or none?

    Answers to these questions have important consequences: (1.1)–(1.4)
ascribe properties to objects of some kind or other. Our conception
of these properties, i.e. our conception of what the truth conditions,
meaning, grammaticality, etc. are, depends on what we believe the
bearers of those properties are. It would be strange, to say the least, to

insist that (1.1) is true, but admit total ignorance about whether the object quoted on its left-hand side is abstract or concrete, a property, an ink mark, or a strange, temporally stretched-out entity.

In sum: this first step in our pro-quotation campaign draws attention to the fact that anyone who cares about the semantics of sentences like (1.1)–(1.4) ought to be embarrassed by not knowing what these sentences say, or not knowing which propositions they express, or not knowing their meanings, or not knowing their truth conditions. You can't, however, know any of these things unless you first understand the nature of quotation.

(b) Opacity

Quotation creates paradigmatic opaque contexts (Quine 1966: 159), indeed, hyperintensional ones, i.e. contexts in which substitution of co-referential or even synonymous expressions fails to preserve truth-value. The inference from (1.4) to (1.5), for example, fails to preserve truth-value (even though 'bachelor' and 'unmarried man', let us suppose, are synonymous).

1.4. 'Bachelor' has eight letters.
1.5. 'Unmarried man' has eight letters.

Opacity is an important topic in philosophy, at least in part, because it is supposed to provide evidence for non-extensional semantic theories. You can't fully understand opacity without understanding quotation. To the extent that opacity issues are significant, it follows that the study of quotation is as well.

Belief reports are standardly invoked as the paradigm of opaque contexts. The inference from (1.6) to (1.7) can, it is often claimed, fail to preserve truth-value, even though Marilyn Monroe is (identical to) Norma Jean Mortenson.

1.6. Jack believes that Marilyn Monroe is a blonde.
1.7. Jack believes that Norma Jean Mortenson is a blonde.

Here's an interesting disanalogy between belief reports and quotation. Some philosophers (e.g. Salmon 1986 and Soames 1989) have argued that the step from (1.6) to (1.7), *contra* intuition, does, and must, preserve truth-value. They claim that the semantic content of (1.6) is true just in case the semantic content of (1.7) is true. The reason most are inclined to deny this, these philosophers speculate, is because they don't distinguish clearly between semantic content and pragmatically conveyed information. Utterances of (1.6) and (1.7) express contents in addition to the propositions that they semantically express and it is only these former contents that can differ in truth-value. By exploiting the semantics–pragmatics distinction, Soames and Salmon try to argue that belief reports are, contrary to first impression, transparent.

This move cannot be dismissed out of hand, as many have been inclined to do, as a sort of cheap and desperate theory-saving maneuver. Granted, as an overall position, it may end up being too costly or having unacceptable consequences, but it is certainly a theoretically interesting move worthy of open-minded philosophical exploration. However, note that the analogous move in connection with quotation would not even be remotely plausible. Anyone who tries to argue that the semantic content of (1.4) is true just in case the semantic content of (1.5) is has not presented us with an intriguing philosophical position we should or would take seriously. In this regard, quotation is the clearest example of an opaque or hyperintensional context we have.

It is worth noting that Davidson's effort to explain (away) the opacity of indirect speech is why he took a particular interest in quotation in the first place. He thought his account of quotation (for example, his account of (1.4) and the direct quotation (1.8)) extended to the indirect quotation (1.9):[2]

1.4. 'Bachelor' has eight letters.
1.8. Quine said, 'Quotation has a certain anomalous feature'.
1.9. Quine said that quotation has a certain anomalous feature.

His own account of the opacity of (1.9) is a cornerstone of his extensional theory of meaning. It enabled him to respond to Fregean arguments against purely extensional meaning theories, i.e. against theories of meaning without a level of meaning in addition to reference. So, should his theory of quotation fail, his extensional theory might fail as well. And if that theory fails, then much of the rest of his philosophy would collapse as well.

In sum: the second step of our pro-quotation campaign consists in pointing out that quotation is perhaps *the* paradigm of an opaque and/or

---

[2] Although the paper on indirect quotation (Davidson 1968) was published long before the one on quotation (Davidson 1979), the latter was written before its publication date. It was circulating in mimeograph form in the 1960s.

hyperintensional context. Opacity has been one of the central topics in philosophy of language—it is one of the issues any theory of meaning and reference must accommodate. If you lack a natural empathy for the study of quotation, then this is the sort of connection that should compel your attention.

(c) The Language–World Connection

One reason why (some) philosophers are interested in language is because they are interested in how language hooks up to the world: how are we able to use language to talk about objects in the world and predicate properties of them? Quotations are used to talk about a very particular part of the world, namely, language itself. So, in the particular case of quotation, the *language–world connection* becomes the *language–language connection*, i.e. quotation is the place where language really does turn on itself.

As we mentioned earlier, there is no agreement about *how* language becomes self-reflective. There is a plethora of theories; according to some, quotations are proper names, demonstratives, indexicals, complex definite descriptions, restricted quantifiers, functors, maybe even predicates, pictures, displays, illustrations, or other peculiar devices. Each theory, accordingly, postulates a different mechanism by virtue of which language turns on itself. As we hinted in the preface, we will endorse the view, contrary to popular opinion, that quotation is a *sui generis* device for connecting language to the world; i.e. the mechanism by which quotations quote cannot be assimilated to familiar devices: e.g. naming, demonstrating, indexing, denoting, quantifying, predicating, or any other known semantic mechanism for connecting language to the world. As such, quotation constitutes one of the most basic ways in which language connects to the world. That's surely interesting.

(d) What Is Said

The notion of *what is said* is a core notion in the philosophy of language. Philosophers as diverse as Kaplan (1989), Davidson (1968), and, of course, Grice (1989) have all committed themselves to the view that no theory of meaning can be developed without accounting for intuitions about what speakers say when they utter sentences. Yet such intuitions, in large part, derive from intuitions about the truth-value of sentences containing the word 'say'.

Quotation marks interact with the verb 'say' in an assortment of important ways. Sentences (1.8)–(1.10) illustrate three important uses of 'say' in English:

   1.8. Quine said 'Quotation has a certain anomalous feature'.
   1.9. Quine said that quotation has a certain anomalous feature.
  1.10. Quine said that quotation 'has a certain anomalous feature'.

Two of these sentences contain quotation marks. One claim we'll examine is whether a unified theory of the way that 'say' functions in reporting sentences (1.8)–(1.10) is possible and if it is, whether such a theory is required. Are there semantic relations among these sentences that require a unified treatment of 'say'? Does an adequate semantic theory of the verb 'say' in *all* its uses require an understanding of the semantics of quotation, so that our understanding of the notion of *what is said* depends, at least in part, on our understanding of quotation?

(e) Compositionality

One central set of questions in twentieth-century philosophy concerned the possibility of constructing compositional meaning theories for natural languages—i.e. finite theories from which the semantic contents of infinitely many natural language sentences are derivable. One reason for this interest is in seeking an explanation of the productivity of natural languages—our capacity for producing, recognizing, and understanding novel sentences in our language is unbounded. In this regard, quotation provides a particular challenge for anyone interested in the project of devising finite compositional meaning theories for natural languages since, for one thing, it enables us to compose novel English sentences out of (an unlimited resource of) quotable items that are not themselves part of the English lexicon. For example, the string (1.11) appears to have as one of its constituents (i.e. 'snøman'), an item that is *not* itself a part of the English lexicon.

  1.11. 'Snøman' isn't a word in English; it's a word of Norwegian.

This is particularly interesting since (1.11) is a true grammatical sentence of English. The problem for compositional meaning theories, then, is this: if some quotable items are not themselves a part of English, and if they are in some sense components of well-formed English sentences that contain them, how then can such grammatical English sentences be built up out of a finite set of meaningful elements *of English*? If there's no such finite set, then how can a finite theory determine the semantic content of all English sentences out of the semantic contents of their constituents?

According to Postal (2004), this feature of quotation presents a serious obstacle for a thesis Noam Chomsky has defended throughout his career. Here are two quotes from Chomsky, one from 1959 and another from 2000 (both in Postal (2004)):

> A language is a collection of sentences of finite length all constructed from a finite alphabet (or, where our concern is limited to syntax, a finite vocabulary) of symbols.   (Chomsky 1959: 137).

> The I-language consists of a computational procedure and a lexicon. The lexicon is a collection of items, each a complex of properties (called 'features') . . . The computational procedure selects items from the lexicon and forms an expression, a more complex array of such features.   (Chomsky 2000: 120).

In both cases, Chomsky assumes that the expressions of a language are constructible from a finite list of symbols (for a number of similar quotes from the rest of Chomsky's corpus, see Postal (2004)). If quotations are expressions in the I-language and can be built out of elements *not* in the lexicon, it's hard to see how the relevant computational procedure can be construed as operating on the lexicon.

Of course, one might respond to this concern by saying that it simply shows that there's a discrepancy, in this respect, between what Chomsky calls I-languages and public languages. If you think, as Chomsky does, that the proper object of study is I-languages, then so much the worse for these allegedly interesting features of quotation. We disagree. Our assumption in what follows is that it will make no difference whether we appeal to public languages or I-languages. We could, for example, use (1.12) as a replacement for (1.11):

> 1.12. 'snøman' is not a word in my idiolect (or: my I-language), but it is in Paul's idiolect (or: I-language).

More generally, the reference to public languages is not essential, we claim, to any of our examples. We're assuming that those who don't believe in public languages can translate our arguments so as to be run on idiolects, I-languages, or whatever your favorite object of study is. How, then, do we respond to the worry that quotation in public languages has features not found in I-languages and that, as Paul Pietroski has suggested (in pers. comm.) to us, 'all metalinguistic discourse is arguably an 'add-on' rather than an illustration of 'core' semantics'? We have no proof that metalinguistic activity is not an add-on, but it seems implausible that it is. Here's some armchair developmental psychology to that effect. A kid who uses 'smatch' to refer to cats will be corrected by something like, 'Cat, not smatch.' It is not entirely implausible to think that this is interpreted by the child as 'That's called a 'cat', not a 'smatch'.'

Of course, many parents are explicitly metalinguistic in the way they talk to and train their children; they'll say things like 'That's called a 'cat'.' Kids seem to understand their parents' instructions. Finally, it seems that what children learn and end up knowing has to be described metalinguistically. They know (and learn) *that 'cats' applies to cats.*

None of this is conclusive evidence, of course, but it does provide some reason for thinking that not only is metalinguistic discourse *not* an add-on, it is among the very core linguistic devices in all natural languages. In some sense, understanding quotation (or some equivalent metalinguistic device) is a precondition for becoming a speaker of a natural language.

(f) The Semantics–Pragmatics Divide

How we answer almost any question in the philosophy of language depends in part on how we draw the distinction between semantic and pragmatic content. Quotation is no exception. Which intuitions are counted as relevant to semantics and which to pragmatics will depend on more general views about how this distinction is most usefully drawn. In earlier work (Cappelen and Lepore 2004), we defend a particular theory of the relationship between semantic and non-semantic content. Quotation affords us an opportunity to apply parts of that general theory to a particularly interesting case. This is one (perhaps the only) point on which we agree with one of our severest critics, namely, Recanati (2001): quotation provides an excellent testing ground for a general theory of the interface between semantic and non-semantic content. We will see these issues surface over and over again in the following chapters. Some illustrations:

- Some claim that so-called mixed quotation (as in (1.10) above; see sect. 2.2) is a non-semantic phenomenon; we disagree.

- Some think that our practice of translating direct quotations reveals something about the semantics of quotation; we disagree and claim that it shows something about the nature of reporting others (where this is different from the semantics of the verb 'to say').

- Some claim that substitution failures in quotational contexts is a semantic phenomenon; we claim that, at least in some cases, it is not.

In all these cases, more general assumptions about how to distinguish semantic from non-semantic content play a central role.

(g) Indexicality, Context Sensitivity, and Monsters

Finally, some authors have thought that quotation challenges the standard view of how indexicals function. The standard view is that the referent of an indexical is fixed *in a context of use*. A token of 'I' refers to whoever tokens it, a token of 'you' refers to the addressee of that token, a token of 'here' refers to the place of that token; a token of 'now' refers to the time of that token, etc. This is a fundamental feature of Kaplan's justly famous paper 'Demonstratives' (1989). Schlenker (2003) summarizes it as what he calls The Fixity Thesis:

> **Fixity Thesis** (a corollary of Direct Reference): The semantic value of an indexical is fixed solely by the context of the actual speech act, and cannot be affected by any logical operators.[3]

Quotation, as we will see below, seems to provide a serious challenge to the Fixity Thesis. Here is an example of a journalist's mixed quotation from Cappelen and Lepore (1997*b*: 429):

> Mr. Greenspan said he agreed with Labor Secretary R. B. Reich 'on quite a lot of things.' Their accord on this issue, he said, has proved 'quite a surprise to both of us.'

Take note of the occurrence of 'us' in the last sentence of this passage; it does *not* refer to the journalist and someone else. Insofar as this example seems to contradict the Fixity Thesis, it should interest anyone studying the nature of context-sensitivity. A study of quotation seems, then, required in order to understand some uses of context-sensitive expressions in some quotations.

---

[3] He takes this to be a corollary of the direct reference principle in Kaplan (1989).

Taking Stock

This completes (for the time being) our public relations effort on behalf of the study of quotation. There are many other interesting philosophical topics we will as a matter of course broach as our study develops. But to wrap matters up thus far: if you are interested in understanding any of (a)–(g), you might want to spend some time thinking about quotation.

- a. the contents of (1.1)–(1.4),
- b. opacity,
- c. the language–world connection,
- d. the notion of what is said,
- e. compositionality,
- f. the semantics–pragmatics distinction, and
- g. the nature of indexicality.

(a)–(g) muster a strong case for the view that quotation is a topic that has received insufficient attention. There are, again to indulge in dubious comparisons, few other topics in the philosophy of language with as puzzling an array of data, and with as many rich entanglements to central issues in the philosophy of language.[4]

---

[4] We are, of course, not claiming that all these issues will be solved just by a proper understanding of the nature of quotation—we're only making the obvious claim that any stand you take on these issues will commit you in various ways to claims about how quotation functions (or at least doesn't function).

2

Preliminaries: 'Quotation' and Varieties of Quotation

Since this book is about quotation, it is natural for you to expect us to provide something like a precise definition or characterization of 'quotation'. To be perfectly frank, at this early stage we can do no better than to identify quotations through examples. We summarize why in the next few subsections. We also introduce some terminology central to our later discussion. We distinguish among four varieties of quotation (without prejudging the scope and limits of our practice of quotation): pure, direct, indirect, and mixed.[1]

2.1. HOW TO DEFINE 'QUOTATION'

2.1.1. Quotation Identified Through Examples

There's an easy and relatively non-controversial way to *identify* a quotation: it is the *sort* of linguistic phenomenon exemplified by the grammatical subject of (1.4) and the grammatical object in (1.8).[2]

1.4. 'Bachelor' has eight letters.
1.8. Quine said 'Quotation has a certain anomalous feature.'

That identification leaves open which semantic and syntactic devices belong to the category of quotation. Any characterization of a more

---

[1] In the appendix to this chapter we also discuss what is called scare quotation. We will claim there it should not be incorporated within a general theory of quotation. Indeed, given the positive views we embrace by the end of this book it will become clear that indirect quotation should be so-called only for historical reasons. It too is a form of speech with no place in a general theory of quotation.

[2] There is some debate about whether the quotation in (1.8) is a grammatical direct object. But nothing hangs on that in the current discussion (see the appendix of Ch. 11 and Munro 1982).

specific nature, either of a syntactic or a semantic sort, we fear, slips into controversy immediately.

2.1.2. Quotation Identified Syntactically

A syntactic characterization of quotation might run something along these lines: take a pair of quotation marks—e.g. single apostrophes in Britain, double apostrophes in the United States, double angles in parts of Europe—and put, for example, a letter, a word, a sentence or any other quotable item between them; what results is a quotation, as in (1.4) and (1.8).

This is a decent definition, but critics have challenged it on three fronts.

a. In spoken language, no obvious correlates of quotation marks exist. Spoken utterances of (2.1) seem often to be *un*accompanied by lexical items corresponding to 'quote/unquote' (Washington 1992: 558).

2.1. My name is Donald.

If you're inclined to hear utterances of (2.1) as quotational, then our syntactic characterization will leave you cold.

b. Even if we restrict our attention to written language, quotations are not invariably indicated by the use of quotation marks. Sometimes, for example, italicization is used instead, as in (2.2):

2.2. *Bachelor* has eight letters.

Other devices employed as substitutes for quotation marks include bold face and indentation (cf. Quine 1940: 23–4; Geach 1957: 82). There's simply no clear or obvious limit on the range of distinct options, other than that they are used as quotation marks, but this, one could argue, renders the syntactic characterization incomplete, and thus, unsatisfactory.

c. Finally, there's a debate about whether this syntactic categorization would be sufficient. Some philosophers claim that so-called 'mixed quotation' is not quotation (for further discussion, see Ch. 6). According to these philosophers, the *syntactic role* of quotation marks varies across sentences—not only is there no unified semantics for all occurrences of quotation marks, there's not even a unified syntax.

We don't think either (a) or (b) is decisive. In reply to (b), we can, not unreasonably, start with sentences containing quotation marks and whatever sits between them, develop a semantic account for these, and then later extend that theory to any other synonymous device. In reply to (a), we will reject the idea that a theory of quotation should accommodate utterances in which there genuinely are no quotation marks (see Ch. 4). We're interested in theories for sentences that contain the syntactic devices ' ' and ' ''; other sentences aren't our concern in this study of quotation. (c), however, presents a worry for an initial classification, since it touches on issues we do not want to prejudge at this stage.

2.1.3. Quotation Identified Semantically

Another tempting strategy for identifying quotations is to go semantic—an item is quoted if it is *mentioned*. At least two problems confront any such suggestion.

a. Several theorists (Washington 1992; Saka 1998; Reimer 2005) want to distinguish between mentioning and quoting. This definition would rule their theories out by stipulation. We don't want to beg any questions at this early stage.

b. A characterization of quotation that appeals to mentioning is no clearer than the distinction between use and mention that it invokes, and matters become complicated as soon as we try to characterize 'mention' and 'use.' Isn't 'bachelor' in (1.4) in some sense *used*? Isn't it used to quote 'bachelor'? If the response is that it is used, but, however, not with its normal semantic value, then we are left with the challenge of defining 'normal' and 'abnormal' semantic values. That, again, leads immediately to controversy that should be avoided at the early stage where we are merely trying to identify our subject matter.

The worries about this semantic characterization of quotation are more convincing than those against the syntactic one. To remain as neutral as possible at this introductory stage, we will stick with a simple identification-through-example strategy for identifying quotations reinforced by the syntactic characterization (with the qualification mentioned above about mixed quotation). We leave open how to characterize quotation semantically; that's better done by a theory of quotation, which is, after all, the central goal of this study.

2.2. VARIETIES OF QUOTATION

In what follows, it will be useful to distinguish among four varieties of quotation that will occupy us in this study—each was illustrated in Ch. 1: *Pure, Direct, Indirect,* and *Mixed* quotation.

   (1.1)–(1.4) are all examples of *pure* quotation.

   1.1. 'Snow is white' is true in English iff snow is white.
   1.2. 'Aristotle' refers to Aristotle.
   1.3. 'The' is the indefinite article in English.
   1.4. 'Bachelor' has eight letters.

In pure quotation, there is no attribution to any utterance or saying event. In this respect, pure quotation differs from direct, mixed, and indirect quotation. Suppose Quine utters sentence (2.3). He can be properly quoted by any of (1.8)–(1.10):

   2.3. Quotation has a certain anomalous feature.
   1.8. Quine said, 'Quotation has a certain anomalous feature'.
   1.9. Quine said that quotation has a certain anomalous feature.
   1.10. Quine said that quotation 'has a certain anomalous feature'.

(1.8) quotes Quine by mentioning words he uttered. This is *direct* quotation. (1.9) quotes him, but could still be true even if Quine hadn't uttered any word in (2.3). This is *indirect* quotation. And (1.10) quotes Quine by reporting what he said, but attributes to him only an utterance of the expression 'has a certain anomalous feature'. This is *mixed* quotation. The category of mixed quotation merits a few additional remarks for anyone unfamiliar with the recent literature on quotation. (It will also be the focus of Ch. 6.)

2.2.1. Mixed Quotation

The first systematic discussion of mixed quotation appears in Davidson (1979). Before his article, the category of mixed quotation was mostly ignored. For the following twenty years, it was still relegated to footnotes in the literature. But during the last ten years or so, it has occupied front row center for anyone interested in quotation. If you think you're unfamiliar with mixed quotation, it is worth observing that in our actual practice of reporting one another's speech, mixed quotation is, arguably, far more common than direct quotation. Peruse any newspaper and one finds reports similar to this, from a *New York Times* article about testimony to a Congressional committee by Chairman of the Federal Reserve, Alan Greenspan:

Greenspan said that some of last year's decline in long-term interest rates 'will have to be refunded'. Passage of a program, by contrast, would bring rates down 'quite a bit further'. He said the Fed would have been 'irresponsible' not to have raised interest rates in 1994 . . . Mr. Greenspan said he agreed with Labor Secretary R. B. Reich 'on quite a lot of things'. Their accord on this issue, he said, has proved 'quite a surprise to both of us'.

There are many reasons for why we go about mixed quoting one another. Here is by no means an exhaustive list of typical reasons for preferring mixed over direct or indirect quotation:

1. The reported utterance is too long to directly quote, but the reporter wants to ensure accuracy on certain key passages (as in the *New York Times* passage).

2. Certain passages in the original utterance were particularly well put (as in: Quine says that quotation 'has a certain anomalous feature').

3. Perhaps the words used by the original speaker were (potentially) offensive to an audience and the speaker wants to distance himself from them by indicating that they are the words of the individual being reported and not his own, as in 'Vice President Dick Cheney on the Senate floor told Senator Patrick Leahy to go 'fuck' himself.'

4. The expressions being mixed quoted might be ungrammatical or a solecism and the speaker might be trying to indicate that he's not responsible; or that he recognizes something is funny or odd about them, as in 'Mary said that John is a wonderful 'philtosopher' ' or 'Howard said that he 'ain't gonna take it no more.' ' (The same sort of point extends to mixed quoting foreign expressions (as in, 'Mario said that he was 'en casa' when the murder occurred').

The relationship between mixed quotation and other varieties of quotation will be pursued in Ch. 6. Our full theory of how the three varieties of quotation connect is presented in Ch. 11.

APPENDIX

Scare-Quoting

This is the first book ever written exclusively on the topic of quotation and metalinguistic representations more generally. Since we want it to cover as much ground as possible, we initially planned to include a chapter about so-called scare-quotes (Geach 1957: 81). It turns out that we don't have much of interest of to say about this phenomenon. What we do have to say are simple variations on points brought out in the discussions of mixed quotation (in Ch. 6) and of impure quotation (in Ch. 5). It also turns out that no other view that we defend in this book depends on what one ends up saying about scare-quoting; it's not a topic that has any bearing whatsoever on the main lines of argumentation here: hence this brief appendix.

In the entire literature on quotation, the only extensive discussions of scare-quoting can be found in two papers by Predelli (2003, 2005). Predelli gives his initial characterization of scare-quoting by quoting the *Chicago Manual of Style*, according to which in some cases it is more appropriate 'to apply a standard technical term in a nonstandard way than to invent a new term . . . in such instances the term is often enclosed in quotation marks.' (2.4) is an example where the speaker intends to indicate that the word 'proofs' is, strictly speaking, misapplied:

> 2.4. In offset printing 'proofs' of illustrations come from the darkroom, not the proof press. (*CMS* 172)

The same applies to slang usage, as in (2.5), where the speaker uses the quotation marks intending to indicate that 'copper's nark' is inappropriate in some way:

> 2.5. Had it not been for Bryce, the 'copper's nark,' Collins would have made his escape. (*CMS* 173)

This sort of distancing also occurs with pejorative terms, as in (2.6):

> 2.6. National greed has disguised itself in mandates to govern 'inferior' races.

According to Predelli, scare-quoting is not a semantic phenomenon (in the sense we use the term 'semantic' here[3]). It's a form of conventional implicature.[4]

---

[3] That, we should point out, is compatible with it contributing to the truth conditions at some level of content being expressed. On our view, utterances succeed in asserting many propositions in addition to their semantic contents (see Cappelen and Lepore 2004, Ch. 13).

[4] Some people use the term 'semantic' so that it includes conventional implicatures, but that is not our usage.

Though that's not incompatible with anything we propose in this book, we're not entirely happy with the category of conventional implicatures and would prefer to classify scare-quoting as *speech act heuristic* (see Cappelen and Lepore 2004). Though a discussion of the nature of conventional implicature and speech act heuristics is interesting, these are topics we choose to bypass here, since extended discussions of the nature of conventional implicatures, etc., would move the book away from its central topic. To see what we have in mind, here are two potentially interesting issues raised by the practice of scare-quoting and our justification for *not* discussing them:

1. It would be interesting from the point of view we're pushing in this book if scare-quoting turned out to be the very same *semantic* phenomenon as pure and direct quotation. That, however, is a view so implausible that it is not worth discussing.

2. A slightly less implausible view would be that scare-quoting and mixed-quotation are, somehow, intimately connected. We take the arguments of Ch. 6 to show that that is not the case. If we are right, the quotes in mixed quotation cannot be dropped. We take Ch. 6 to prove that conclusively. In scare-quoting they can be dropped without a loss of semantic content (at least according to every theory of scare-quoting in print that we know about). So, they are two different phenomena. If, on the other hand, someone were to suggest that the quotes in scare-quotation *cannot* be dropped, then, presumably, whatever we say about mixed-quotation will help you understand scare-quoting. Again, this makes a separate discussion of the phenomenon less pressing.

None of this is to say that there's nothing interesting to be said about our practice of scare-quoting. On the contrary, Predelli's papers show that this can be a rich area of study.

PART I

DATA

Chapters 8–11 discuss and evaluate a number of theories of quotation. Many of the arguments in these chapters take the form: Theory of Quotation T fails because it can't explain feature f of quotation. Rather than pulling features out of our hats, it will make for an easier read if we first describe the data in as theoretically a neutral way as possible. That's the goal of Chs. 3–7. These chapters describe *some* features quotations (are alleged to) have. After examining the literature, we have settled on a list of twelve data (D1)–(D12) that have been significant in driving the published discussion on quotation. This list is not exhaustive—indeed, other conditions will arise naturally in the course of discussing why one account or another fails. Why a particular adequacy condition should be respected may only become clear when it is placed in the context of a failed account.

3

Overview

In this chapter we will arduously avoid entering into controversy. Rather, we will simply present the central data, (D1)–(D12), and leave their correct interpretations for later chapters. All that we insist upon, in this chapter, is that an adequate theory of quotation say *something* about how to accommodate the data surrounding (D1)–(D12).

D1. OPACITY

In Ch. 1, we maintained that an interest in opacity should trigger an interest in quotation. This is reflected in adequacy condition (D1): In quotation neither coextensive nor synonymous expressions can be substituted for one another *salva veritate*. An inference from (1.4) to (1.5), for example, fails to preserve truth-value.

> 1.4. 'Bachelor' has eight letters.
> 1.5. 'Unmarried man' has eight letters.

No theory of quotation is adequate unless it respects opacity and no theory of opacity is complete until it explains why quotation exhibits this feature; a theory of quotation must go further, since it must explain opacity but also hyperintensionality—that is, it must explain why in quotational contexts synonyms cannot be substituted for one another *salva veritate*.

D2. QUANTIFYING IN

It is not possible to quantify into quotation *salva veritate*. Sentence (3.1), for example, does not follow from (1.4):

1.4. 'Bachelor' has eight letters.
3.1. (∃x)('x' has eight letters).[1]

When we try to quantify into (1.4) using an existential quantifier with a variable 'x', the product of quoting 'x' is an expression that quotes the 24th letter of the Roman alphabet; quotation marks, at least in English, cannot be quantified into without trapping the variable. In this regard, to the extent that we can make sense of (3.1) it is an example of vacuous quantification over a sentence that quotes that very variable. A theory of quotation should explain why that is so.

D3. INFINITUDE

No upper bound exists on the number of quotations there are in English. With concatenations of the letter 'a' alone we can generate an infinite list of quotations. So understanding the mechanism of quotation requires mastering an infinite capacity, a capacity to understand and generate a potential infinity of new quotations. We don't learn quotations one by one. Never having encountered the quotation in (3.2) before does not prohibit comprehending it (Christensen 1967: 362) and identifying what it quotes.

3.2. 'Asdlier' is not a word of English.

Similarly, there seems to be no upper bound on a speaker's capacity for generating novel quotations. A theory of quotation should explain how this can be so.

D4. EXTANT LEXICON

Quotation is not limited to an extant lexicon or list of familiar symbols. Quotation is different from any other linguistic device in this regard

---

[1] Of course, there could be a formal language that works like this but English doesn't: notice that even though (3.1) has a formalized existential quantifier, and so is not an expression of English, sentence (3.1.1) is a bona fide attempt at an English sentence, and it fares no better.

3.1.1. There is a thing and 'it' has eight letters.

inasmuch as it doesn't operate exclusively on a fixed lexicon of the language. It reaches beyond the lexicon in at least three distinct respects:

1. We can, in English, quote items from languages other than English. (1.11) is perfectly intelligible:

    1.11. 'Snøman' isn't a word in English; it's a word in Norwegian.

2. We can, in English, quote gibberish, i.e. combinations of linguistic items that don't mean anything in any natural language. (3.3) is an example.

    3.3. 'Kqxf' is not a meaningful linguistic expression (Wertheimer 1999: 515).

3. We can even quote (basic) units that are not part of the language or the sign system[2] we typically use. We can, for example, introduce novel symbols, as in (3.4):

    3.4. '☺' will be stamped on the forehead of every semantic minimalist.

This is fairly uncontroversial.

Are there limits on what can be quoted? There's disagreement about that among theorists, and intuitions seems to differ on this issue. Bennett for one writes in a criticism of Davidson:

[Davidson's view] seems to imply that it would be a proper use of quotation to write: At the very end of his letter, after his name but on the same line, he put ' ', with a picture of a face, or a shapeless black blob, or a sketch of the Taj Mahal, between the quotation marks . . . I don't think it is correct. One might occasionally put a scrawl or doodle between quotation marks, and be understood to have referred to its shape, but only as a joking extension of conventional quotation. (Bennett 1988: 405)

In order to test intuition about these issues, ask yourself whether you find the following comprehensible:

3.5. '🐶' is a picture of a dog, not a Chinese symbol.

3.6. '༘' is a symbol used by Martians.

3.7. '⚘' is not a word in John's handwriting; it's a wingding.

If (3.5)–(3.7) are intelligible, then, contra Bennett, doodles, scribbles, and pictures can be quoted. Bennett goes on to make an interesting

---

[2] We will elaborate on the notion of a sign system in Ch. 12.

observation about the implications of endorsing a liberal view about the scope of quotation:

> If I don't know what features of inscriptions are significant in Martian, my grasp of any quotation of a Martian expression is essentially fragile. I can indeed extract information from it, but not in the way I do from quotations that I properly understand. Evidence for this: the only way I can safely pass the information along is by writing a perfect replica of the item my information displayed in his quotation, like the tailor who when told to copy a suit reproduced the tear in its sleeve. In other words, I can convey the information only by passing along my whole basis for it; and that shows that I am operating on something I don't really understand.   (*Ibid.* 407–8)

If (3.5)–(3.7) are intelligible, then Bennett's remark is appropriate, not as an *objection* (as he sees it), but rather as a keen observation about what it takes to understand quotation. If these sentences are intelligible, it may not be a requirement for understanding (3.5)–(3.7) that you know exactly which features are relevant. Similarly, to understand (3.8), you may not need to know the relevant features of Apple Chancery.

3.8. 'L' is in the font Apple Chancery.

Perhaps this sentence is your introduction to the font—it may be the way in which, after a while, you come to learn how to reproduce items in this font.

As noted above, we don't want to take a stand at this stage on just how far the range of quotable items reaches (whether, for example, it includes Martian symbols, symbols we don't know the relevant features of), but any adequate theory of quotation would have to take a stand on these and related issues. Our own view of these issues is presented in Ch. 12, where we articulate how we think it is best to delineate the scope and limits of quotable items—both on the epistemological question about what we need to know to competently employ a quotation expression and on the metaphysical question about the individuation conditions for quotation expressions and the quotable items they quote.

D5. THE PROXIMITY CONSTRAINT AND THE DISQUOTATIONAL SCHEMA

There's a particularly close relationship between a quotation and its semantic value, one like no other kind of expression bears to its semantic values. Compare the relationship between the quotation expression ' 'Quine' ' and its semantic value, namely, the name 'Quine', with the relationship between the latter and its semantic value, namely, the great American philosopher of the twentieth century. The point we have in mind here is difficult to make precise and non-metaphorical. Nonetheless, it is immediately striking to anyone who contemplates our practice of quotation for more than a moment. ' 'Quine' ' and 'Quine' are intimately related in a way that 'Quine' and Quine are not. The quotation expression (i.e. ' 'Quine' ') has its semantic value, i.e. the item it quotes ('Quine'), contained within it, (in a sense of 'contain' to be made more precise in Chs. 11 and 12) but the semantic value of 'Quine', i.e. the philosopher, is nowhere to be found in 'Quine'. Were it there, confrontations with that expression would be a lot more interesting than they are.

Other authors couch this point in different ways. Here are three characterizations from the literature:

1. . . . a quotation somehow pictures what it is about (Davidson 1979: 82).
2. A quotation is . . . a *hieroglyph* . . . [that] designates its object . . . by picturing it (Quine 1940: 26).
3. . . . we can go from knowing the quotation of any expression to knowing the expression itself (Saka 1998: 116).[3]

We ourselves prefer to speak vaguely (at this stage) of the quotation expression *containing* whatever item it quotes. In Ch. 11, we will propose that this idea of containment be taken *literally*, but at this stage, all we will assume is that a theory of quotation must explain (or explain away) our intuitions, however vague or imprecise, about the special nature of this relationship.

The point about proximity is related to what we shall call the Disquotational Schema for Quotation (QS):

> **QS:** ' 'e' ' quotes 'e'

(where replacing 'e' in QS in both of its occurrences with any quotable item yields a truth[4]). Indeed, it looks as though an even stronger

---

[3] See also Bennett (1988: 401) who writes of a quotation expression that 'what is displayed in a quotation is systematically related to what it names.'

[4] Looking ahead to Ch. 11, we will use QS as an axiom schema for interpreting quotation expressions and claim that it exhausts the semantic contribution of quotation.

principle correctly characterizes our practice of quotation; we call this the Strong Disquotational Schema (SDS):

   (SDS) Only ' 'e' ' quotes 'e'

(where 'e' is replaceable by any quotable item). For example, the semantics for quotation seems to make it impossible to use ' 'Jason' ' to quote 'Quine'.

Even though intuitively obvious, SDS is still remarkable. We all grew up being taught that it is a truism that the relationship between a linguistic expression and its semantic value is completely *arbitrary,* outside, perhaps, of a few examples of onomatopoeia. No name must name what it as a matter of fact names; it could have been used to name something else. No predicate must apply to whatever it applies to; it might have been used to apply to something else. And so on for the rest of our linguistic repertoire. This arbitrariness is treated as almost definitional of what it is to be a linguistic expression. But quotation, however, shows that this *arbitrariness* is not an essential feature of the relationship between all expressions and their semantic values. No quotation *could* have quoted anything other than what it as a matter of fact quotes. In some significant sense of 'arbitrary' this means that the relationship is anything but arbitrary. We'll return to this intriguing feature of quotation in Ch. 12.

SDS is obviously closely related to proximity; the reason why ' 'Jason' ' can't quote 'Quine' is because the two do not stand in the relevant intimate relationship to each other (regardless of whether this gets spelled out as in (1), (2), (3) or in our preferred way invoking containment).[5]

D6. SYNTACTIC CHAMELEONISM

A number of authors have committed themselves to all quotations being noun phrases. Simchen concludes that in (1.10) the quoted words must be 'Both used and mentioned, *on pain of ungrammaticality*—judging by its position with the whole sentence, the quotation in [(1.10)] cannot be employed simply as a singular term in the mentioning of Quine's

---

[5] Note: there is no worry about using ' 'Jason' ' to name 'Quine'; someone could introduce a new name into the language that begins with the left quote followed by the name 'Jason' followed by the right quote; our point is that this relationship, although it can be a naming relation, cannot be quotation.

words' (Simchen 1999: 326, emphasis our own; cf. also Saka 1998: 120, 127). We want to deny this. So, consider the occurrences of ' 'has a certain anomalous feature' ' in (3.9)–(3.10) and (1.10).

3.9. 'has a certain anomalous feature' is not a complete sentence.
3.10. Quine said 'has a certain anomalous feature'.
1.10. Quine said that quotation 'has a certain anomalous feature'.

The syntactic category of ' 'has a certain anomalous feature' ' in these three sentences is *not* obviously the same. The quotation expression in (3.9), we agree, is its grammatical subject, and thereby must be a noun phrase. But in (3.10) it's unclear what its syntactic status is. On its face, it looks to be the direct object of the verb 'said', and so it should be a noun phrase, but on second glance it would seem that the story is more complicated.

For an ordinary transitive verb, say, 'boils', we cannot substitute the direct object for the subject and preserve meaning: namely, although (3.11) and (3.12) are grammatical, they don't mean the same thing.

3.11. John boiled the water.
3.12. The water boiled John.

But exchanging the quotation in (3.10) with its subject does not change meaning, as in (3.13):

3.13. 'has a certain anomalous feature' said Quine.

This data suggests a more complicated story about the syntactic status of quotations in direct quotations (see the appendix in Ch. 11 for further discussion).

As for (1.10), it's fair to say that no one has a clue as to its syntactic status. If we treat it as a noun phrase (NP), it looks as if we are committed to the syntactic shape of (1.10) being something along the lines of:

$$*[NP_1 \ [V \ [COMP \ [NP_2 \ NP_3]_S]_{CP}]_{VP}]_S$$

But the complement clause CP in this structure is flawed, since concatenating two noun phrases does not make a sentence; NP_3 should be a verb phrase (and not a noun phrase), and so calls into question the status of the quotation expression in (1.10) as a noun phrase. Note: we say 'calls into question' and not 'disproves.' We will develop the idea that the quotation expression in (1.10) is a verb phrase (and not a noun phrase) in Ch. 11.

Minimally, what these data indicate is that quotation is a strange sort of syntactic beast—a *syntactic chameleon*—apparently taking on distinct syntactic roles in distinct linguistic environments. A theory of quotation must say something—one way or the other—about the apparent syntactic flexibility of quotation expressions.

D7. SIMULTANEOUS USE AND MENTION IN MIXED QUOTATION

As noted in Ch. 1, Davidson (1979) claims that in (1.10) the quoted words are both used *and* mentioned.[6]

1.10. Quine said that quotation 'has a certain anomalous feature'.

According to Davidson, (1.10) is simultaneously used to say what Quine said and to say that he used the words 'has a certain anomalous feature' in saying it.

Daniel Seymour (1996: 309) believes expressions inside quotations—both mixed and direct—retain their semantic properties and he bases his view on the occurrence outside a quotation of (co-referential) words that substitute anaphorically for an element inside the quotation. He writes: '[. . .] such examples as 'Jones said ' 'Smith rules the moon', and he does' cannot guarantee that 'he' picks up Smith as its referent instead of the word 'Smith' if the words occurring in the quotational context are not interpreted.'

The co-reference between ' 'Smith' ' and 'he' can only be explained, according to Seymour, if the normal interpretation of 'Smith' remains accessible within the quotation. Any theory that blocks this interpretation automatically, he claims, leaves unexplained the numerous cases of 'semantic dependency between quoted and unquoted material' (D. Seymour 1996: 314).

How a theory should account for these data about alleged uses of words inside quoted material is controversial. We will argue (contrary to Cappelen and Lepore 1997*b*) in Chs. 6 and 11 that no corresponding

---

[6] Partee (1973: 411) also discusses the phenomenon but does not go on to theorize about it since, according to her, 'such sentences do not occur in ordinary spoken language.' We disagree. Were you to hear someone utter,

John said with a heavy Jersey accent that he 'ain't gonna take it no more'

you would almost certainly take some of the material after 'he' to be mixed quoted.

indirect report of Quine's follows from the semantic content of (1.10) (i.e. it doesn't follow from (1.10) that Quine said that quotation has a certain anomalous feature). (1.10), however, can't be true unless Quine said something about quotation. We further argue that the words *inside the quotation* in a mixed (and direct) quotation sentence are never used, despite whatever apparent linguistic relations obtain between the quoted items and anaphoric pronouns (and other linguistic phenomena).

What we just told you is a preview—in very broad brush strokes—of the theory we intend to develop in later chapters—we certainly will not want to claim that this is part of the initial data. The initial data seems to indicate that there's some kind of simultaneous use and mention in mixed quotation. There are three kinds of reaction one might have to this data: one might

1. present a theory that supports the initial intuition, i.e. a theory according to which the semantics for a mixed quotation require that the quoted words be both used and mentioned;

2. deny the initial intuition by saying that in mixed quotation, the semantic content doesn't recognize quotation marks—at the semantic level the quotation marks are superfluous;

3. deny the initial intuition by saying that in mixed quotation, the semantic content doesn't imply that the quoted words are used—only quoted.

Positions (1) and (2) have been defended in print by many authors; (3) is novel to this book. Position (1) is clearly intuitive, but any proponent of either (2) or (3) has some explaining to do. We'll argue in Chs. 6 and 11 against (1) and (2) and in defense of (3).

D8. INDEXICALS INSIDE MIXED QUOTATION

In Ch. 1, we drew your attention to a peculiarity of the apparent behavior of indexical expressions inside mixed quotations. Here is the example we used there of a journalist's mixed quotation from Cappelen and Lepore (1997*b*: 429):

> Mr. Greenspan said he agreed with Labor Secretary R. B. Reich 'on quite a lot of things'. Their accord on this issue, he said, has proved 'quite a surprise to both of us'.

Take note of the occurrence of 'us' in the last sentence of this passage; it does *not* refer to the journalist and someone else.[7] Two examples from Cumming (2005) make this point even clearer:

(C1) Bush also said his administration would 'achieve our objectives' in Iraq. (*New York Times*, 4 November 2004)

(C2) He now plans to make a new, more powerful absinthe that he says will have 'a more elegant, refined taste than the one I'm making now.'

Try removing the quotation marks from (C1) and (C2) and the results are (C1*) and (C2*):

(C1*) Bush also said his administration would achieve our objectives in Iraq.

(C2*) He now plans to make a new, more powerful absinthe that he says will have a more elegant, refined taste than the one I'm making now.

What this shows it that *if* in a mixed quotation, the quoted part is both used and mentioned, then to retrieve what was said, you cannot merely remove the quotation marks. The relevant indirect report (if there is one) can't be obtained simply by stripping off the quotation marks. How mixed quotes should be interpreted is a matter of theory (and issues that will be discussed extensively in Chs. 6 and 11).

D9: CONTEXT SENSITIVITY (OR INDETERMINACY OR AMBIGUITY) IN QUOTATION

One widespread view is that quotations are context-sensitive or ambiguous or indeterminate. That is, one and the same quotation can, on this view, quote a number of distinct items on different occasions of use, all contingent upon the context of utterance. García-Carpintero (1994: 261) illustrates this kind of view and the kind of argument typically given for it. He says that the quotation ''gone'' can quote any of the following:

---

[7] This observation has been emphasized to us by Cumming (2005). Although he uses it to defend an account other than our own, he brought us to see clearly the significance of this data.

- The expression (''gone' is dissyllabic');
- Different types instantiated by the tokens ('*gone*' is cursive');
- Different types somehow related to the token (say, the graphic version of the uttered quoted material, or the spoken version of the inscribed quoted material, as in ''gone' sounds nice');
- Different tokens somehow related to the quoted token ('What was the part of the title of the movie which, by falling down, caused the killing?—'gone' was');
- The quoted token itself ('At least one of these words is heavier than 'gone'' which you should imagine written in big wooden letters).

Others think quotations can quote contents or concepts. Goldstein (1984: 4) says: 'For when Elvis says 'Baby, don't say 'don't',' he is not just requiring his baby to refrain, when confronted with a certain request, from uttering tokens of the same phonetic shape as 'don't', but from uttering any tokens that *mean* the same.' Similarly, the alleged ambiguity of quotation plays an important role in Saka's theory of quotation (discussed further in Ch. 8). According to Saka, quotations can serve the purpose of directing the speaker's attention to 'some object saliently associated with the expression other than its extension' (Saka 1998: 123). This salient object can be a wide variety of things: a token (3.14), a type (3.15), words understood as form–content pairings (3.16); lexemes understood as words abstracted from their inflectional paradigms (3.17); forms, that is, spellings or pronunciations (3.18); and content both immediate (3.19) and translated (3.20) (*ibid.*; our numbering):

3.14. 'I' refers to me.
3.15. 'I' does not refer to anyone in particular; only tokens of it do.
3.16. 'Run' is used in the third-person plural but not singular.
3.17. 'Run' refers to run, runs, ran, running.
3.18. 'Run' consists of three letters.
3.19. The concept 'premise' is the same as the concept 'premiss'.
3.20. Galileo (who spoke no English) said 'The Earth moves!'

If quotation exhibits this kind of flexibility, theories of quotation would all have to be evaluated according to whether they could accommodate it or not.[8] We, however, don't find any of these arguments any good.

---

[8] Geach (1957: 80) speaks of direct quotation—'oratio recta'—as 'used metaphorically to report what somebody thought, 'said in his heart' (without, of course implying that the thinker had the quoted words in his mind)'.

For reasons that will become clear in Ch. 7, we disagree sharply with this interpretation of the data. The final analysis is complex and rather messy. In the end (Ch. 12), our view will be that there is neither semantic ambiguity nor context sensitivity nor semantic indeterminacy in quotation.

D10. ITERABILITY IN QUOTATION

A number of authors argue that a theory of quotation must explain why quotation is (seemingly) iterable. Typically, speakers adopt the following quotation convention: double quotation marks (as in ' 'lobster' ') quote a single quotation expression (i.e. 'lobster'). Three quotation marks (as in ' ' 'lobster' ' ') quote a double quotation expression (i.e. ' 'lobster' '); and so on. This practice seems to support the view that quotation is a semantically iterative device in the sense of Iteration:

> **Iteration**: The semantic value of an n-level quotation is a function (the result) of the semantic value of the corresponding n-1 level quotation being placed inside a pair of matching quote marks.

(where an n-level quotation is a quotation with n matching left and right quotation marks). So, for example, Saka writes:

> Just as we can refer to the word in (11), a verb, by means of forming the metaword in (12), a noun phrase, we can refer to the word in (12) by means of forming the metametaword in (13), ad infinitum. (It is clear that quotations are noun phrases, as they function as grammatical subjects.):
> (11) Sit
> (12) 'Sit'
> (13) ' 'Sit' '
> (Saka 1998: 119–20; cf., also, Reimer 1996, and Washington 1992)

Saka evokes this alleged fact about quotation in criticizing various theories of quotation. He argues, for example, that Davidson's Demonstrative Theory of quotation (which we discuss in Ch. 10) cannot accommodate Iteration. We will return to this topic in Chs. 10–12.

D11. QUOTATION WITHOUT QUOTATION MARKS

Some theorists think quotation marks are not required for quotation. According to Washington (1992), when he introduces himself to someone by uttering, 'Hi, my name is Corey,' there need be no elliptical quotation marks in the sentence, nor any quotation marks hidden in its logical form. Nonetheless, the sentence is grammatical and true (for the reasons you think it is true, i.e. because Corey's name is 'Corey'.) What's going on, according to Washington, is that he is using 'Corey' *quotationally.*

According to theorists who share Washington's view a central task for a theory of quotation is to explain this kind of *quotational use* and relate it to the use of quotation with quotation marks. We discuss this issue in Ch. 4.

D12. 'IMPURE' DIRECT QUOTES

Here's an indisputable fact about our practice of direct quotation. We treat sentences like (3.21) and (3.22) as if they are true:

3.21. Descartes said that man 'is a thinking substance'.
3.22. Frege said that predicate expressions 'are unsaturated'.

We treat these as true even though Descartes said what he said in French or Latin and Frege in German. How can we truly attribute words to speakers who never uttered those words? A theory of quotation should address that issue. Chapter 5 is devoted to a more careful analysis of these and related data.

SUMMARY: (D1)–(D12) AS ADEQUACY CONDITIONS

We have completed our preliminary canvass of the central desiderata on a theory of quotation. Other adequacy conditions will arise naturally in the course of the discussion that follows, particularly in response to criticisms of various theories of quotation. Still, for the rest of this book, we will regularly refer back to (D1)–(D12) with the following constraint:

> A theory of quotation must either explain how quotations can exhibit features (D1)–(D12), or, if it fails to do so, it must present an argument for why an unexplained feature requires no explanation.

Before we introduce, develop and evaluate various theories of quotation, we devote the next few chapters to a more careful discussion of (D7), (D8), (D9), (D11), and (D12). With those discussions in hand, we'll be able to evaluate various theories of quotation more easily in later chapters.

4

Omitted Quotation Marks

In the next four chapters we discuss interpretations of some of the data points canvassed in the previous chapter. In this chapter, we consider the phenomenon of omitted quotation marks (D11). Some theorists hold that quotation marks (or any other linguistic indicator) are *un*required for quotation. We examine the data allegedly in support of this claim because it will play a central role in evaluating so-called Use Theories of Quotation in Ch. 8.

Some theorists argue that the data surrounding our practice of mixed quotation establish that it is not a real form of quotation (and in so doing they present a particular interpretation of (D7) and (D8). In particular, these theorists argue that quotation marks in mixed quotes can be dropped without a loss of meaning. What these data are and what their various interpretations are will be critically examined in Ch. 5. The result of that examination will play an important role in our positive theory in Ch. 11, and, indirectly, in our discussion of Use Theories in Ch. 8.

In Ch. 6, we discuss (D12), the claim that translational and other 'impure' direct quotes are important for an understanding of quotation. Our discussion of that point will play an important role in our discussion of context sensitivity in Ch. 7 and indirectly in our positive view in Ch. 11.

Finally, in Ch. 7, we return to the question of the alleged context sensitivity/ambiguity/indeterminacy of quotation (i.e. (D9)). We will argue that, contrary to what we ourselves once defended (Cappelen and Lepore 1997*b*), quotation is none of these. That conclusion will play an important role in our criticism both of Use Theories, in Ch. 8, and Davidson's theory, in Ch. 9.

4.1. DATA ABOUT OMITTING QUOTATION MARKS, THE QUESTION, AND OPPOSING VIEWS

Are quotation marks necessary for quotation? You might have thought the answer is obviously, if not definitionally, 'yes'. Quine thought as much when he wrote: 'it would be not merely untrue but ungrammatical and meaningless to write: Dreary rhymes with weary' (Quine 1959: 38). But not everyone agrees with Quine. Washington (1992: 588), for example, says:

In conversation, oral promptings ('quote-unquote') or finger-dance quotes can often be omitted without impairing the intelligibility or well-formedness of the utterance. When I introduce myself, I do not say 'My name is quote-unquote Corey,' nor do I make little finger gestures or even use different intonation in order to show that it is my name and not myself that is being talked about.

Saka (1998: 118), commenting on this very passage from Washington, writes:

The point can be made even stronger, I might add. Quote marks are often omitted in writing as well (contra Reimer 1996): it is downright *normal*, outside of scholarly writing, to exclude quote marks, especially in constructions like 'The word cats is a noun'; and even in logic publications, where one might expect the greatest exactitude, it is common for quote marks to be omitted.

According to Reimer (1996: 135), 'any view of quotation that regards the quotation marks as an essential part of the referring expression is mistaken' (for further comments along these same lines, see Recanati 2001, Benbaji 2004*a*, 2004*b*, and Wertheimer 1999: 516). In regard to these data, we are supposed to conclude that a theory of quotation based solely on expressions with quotation *marks* is incomplete. It is incomplete because quotation doesn't require quotation marks. You *can* use 'cat' to quote 'cat' without using quotation marks.[1] If this is a real possibility, then clearly there must be a special quotational use of language because, normally used, the word 'cat' applies to felines and not to an expression. If it can also be used to talk about the word 'cat', then there must be at least two different ways to use 'cat'—its normal

---

[1] Saka (1998) prefers to say that when there are no quotation marks the expression is 'mentioned': Nothing we have to say in what follows will hang on this terminological issue.

way and its quotational way. With the latter, a speaker succeeds in talking about the expression itself.[2]

This line of thought has led to the development of what we shall call 'Use Theories of Quotation'—theories that postulate a special 'quotational usage' of language. The goal of this chapter, however, is to address the relevant data—to investigate whether it is possible to quote without quotation marks. Our conclusions here will be used to refute Use Theories in Ch. 8.

The alleged legitimate uses of sentences (4.1)–(4.5) are the kinds of cases that motivate the quotation-without-quotation-marks view about quotation:

4.1. Cats is a noun.   [spoken]
4.2. Hello is a salutation.   [spoken]
4.3. My name is Corey.
4.4. Donald is Davidson's name.
4.5. Love is a four-letter word.

These sentences give rise to the following three questions (A)–(C):

(A) Are (4.1)–(4.5) grammatical?
(B) Can they semantically express the same propositions as (4.1*)–(4.5*)?
4.1*. 'Cats' is a noun.
4.2*. 'Hello' is a salutation.
4.3*. My name is 'Corey'.
4.4*. 'Donald' is Davidson's name.
4.5*. 'Love' is a four-letter word.
(C) If the answers to (A) and (B) are 'yes', does it follow that a semantics for quotation that applies only to sentences containing quotation marks (or their equivalents) is somehow incomplete or mistaken?

Call the view that answers all of (A), (B), and (C) affirmatively the QWQ Thesis (short for 'Quotation Without Quotation Marks'). The goal of this chapter is to present evidence against QWQ. We show first that the answer to (C) is 'no', and then, that the answers to both (A) and (B) are 'no' as well.

---

[2] Or something related to it, see further discussion of Use Theories in Ch. 8.

4.2. ANSWER TO (C)

Here's what's going on with (C), as far as we can tell. Most authors who have written on quotation over the past one hundred years have been trying to develop a semantic theory for sentences with quoted expressions, i.e. sentences with expressions surrounded by quotation marks. Suppose (4.1)–(4.5) are sentences without quotation marks at any level of logical analysis (i.e. suppose no quotation marks are hidden in deep structure or are in some other way unarticulated). Suppose further that (4.1)–(4.5) can be used to talk about expressions, i.e. suppose that the answers to (A) and (B) are both 'yes.' What follows? Not much, as far as we can tell. Here's what a traditional semanticist about the inextricability of quotation from quotation marks should say:

The theory of quotation doesn't explain all sorts of things. In addition to not explaining quotational usage without quotation marks it also doesn't explain why penguins can't fly or why naked mole rats are blind. It's not meant to explain this other stuff. It's a theory about sentences with expressions surrounded by quotation marks. That's what we have opted to call 'quotation', but we're not wedded to the expression; the Use Theorist can have it if he wants to construe quotation more broadly.

Our point: you cannot aim for (because you cannot have) a unified theory of metalinguistic talk, i.e. of talk about language. If you use the word 'quotation' to refer to any way in which language can be used to talk about language, it is obvious, then, that there can't be a unified theory of quotation. Consider (4.6)–(4.9):

4.6. The first word in this sentence is the definite article in English.
4.7. That letter is pretty.
4.8. Some words are more interesting than others
4.9. 'Alice swooned' is used as an example by Davidson.

It is indisputable that there will be no *unified* semantics for all these metalinguistic uses. In other words, if you want to use the word 'quotation' to refer to all talk *about* language, then you can't have a unified theory of quotation.

As we see it, if we can talk about language in the ways that Washington and Saka opine we can, then that just means there's another way of talking about language, a way traditional theories of quotation were never meant to cover. Anyone is free to develop a theory of this other way of talking about language but it is not in competition with a theory of quotation (since it is not trying to explain what a theory of quotation is trying to explain). So our answer to (C) is 'no'.

According to the view we're arguing against, if quotation marks are to have any essential semantic role to play in a language, semantic theories would have to posit implicit marks when they are absent (Washington 1992). Our reply to this position is that we needn't posit missing quotation marks. That is the chief misunderstanding behind this objection. If no quotation marks are there, we needn't worry about them in trying to develop a semantic theory for sentences *with* quotation marks.

4.2.1. A Possible Counter-Reply

In response, someone might counter: You're right; we can't have a unified treatment of (4.6)–(4.9). But the cases we have in mind are unlike these. They are like (4.1)–(4.5), and these really do include *quoted* expressions, just not quotation marks; they are *just like* sentences with quotation marks except minus the quotation marks. And a semantic theory for quotation *should* explain what goes on in these cases as well.

It's the 'just like' and the 'should' parts we disagree with. If our opponents are right, and there are no quotation marks in (4.1)–(4.5) (something we're *not* granting at this point, but going along with for the sake of argument), then that's a good reason for concluding that these are *not* like sentences with quotation marks and if they aren't, then our theory shouldn't accommodate them.

A proponent of the possibility of 'genuine' quotation without quotation marks might reply: Suppose we have two theories: T1 provides a unified account of pure, direct, mixed quotation cases *and* of (4.1)–(4.5) as well, while T2 provides a unified account of only the first three (and then invokes a different theory to account for (4.1)–(4.5). Shouldn't we prefer T1 over T2? Isn't that what's going on here? Aren't you aspiring to a theory less explanatorily powerful than one that can explain (4.1)–(4.5) (and maybe lots of other things as well, including scare-quotes, open quotation, etc.)?

We have two comments about an appeal to unity (or to a more explanatorily powerful theory).

No one who has run the omitted quotation marks objection has yet to proffer a unified account of so-called quotation without quotation marks together with quotation with quotation marks. All the theories that focus on the quotation without quotation marks provide a separate independent semantics for quotation with quotation marks. So, unification has never been pursued by anyone (suggesting that considerations of unification can't be the underlying concern here). Here are two examples, one from Saka and one from Recanati (both proponents of the possibility of 'genuine quotation without quotation-marks').

Syntactically, a pair of quote marks is a discontinuous determiner (a complex symbol which, applied to an argument expression, produces a noun phrase). Semantically, a pair of quote marks is a concept or intension, QUOT, which ambiguously or indeterminately maps its argument expression X into some linguistic item saliently associated with X other than the extension of X. Although quote marks generally do not specify among token, type, form, and concept, they still serve to partially disambiguate, for they rule out customary reference as the intended interpretation. Thus, the speaker who uses quote marks announces 'I am not (merely) using expression X but am mentioning it.'   (Saka 1998: 127)

Clearly, this is not an account of quotation without quotation marks (what Saka calls 'mention'; see *ibid.* 126).

What we, for the sake of argument, have called 'quotation with quotation marks', Recanati calls 'closed quotation', and about closed quotation he says:

Whenever a linguistic demonstration (a quotation) is linguistically recruited in this way and serves as a singular term, filling a slot in the sentence, I say the quotation is *closed*.   (Recanati 2001: 649)

Quotations can also, and often do, contribute directly to truth-conditional content. That happens whenever a quotation is closed, that is, linguistically recruited as a singular term in the mentioning sentence. Because it functions as a regular singular term, both syntactically and semantically, closed quotation undoubtedly is a genuine linguistic phenomenon.   (*ibid.* 683)

What Recanati writes here makes it very clear that the semantics for closed quotation is different from the other cases of what he calls 'open quotation'—which includes cases of quotation without quotation marks.

In other words, these two authors do not attempt to put a unified theory on the table, and so it cannot be the issue of unity that motivates their focus on quotation-mark-free quotation. We have to admit, we're not sure what their motivation is.

We have a second comment about an appeal to unity. Theorists who claim that quotation without quotation marks is possible, sentences like (4.10) are deemed acceptable (see e.g. Saka 1998 and Reimer 1996):

4.10. Alice is a noun.

According to this view, (4.10) can be used to mean either (4.11) or (4.12):

4.11. The girl, Alice, is a noun.
4.12. The expression, 'Alice', is a noun.

Note that the *only* way to disambiguate a use of (4.10) (on the assumption it has two readings, something we disbelieve but concede for the sake of argument) is to use quotation marks, as we did in (4.12). Notice that an interesting fact about (4.12) is that you can't remove its quotation marks without incurring a further ambiguity. This is because Alice, the girl, could be an expression: after all, it's in principle possible to use people as words, and in such circumstances Alice, the girl, could be a noun. So quotation marks play a role in disambiguation; a role that their non-quotation-marked quotational counterparts cannot play. This is another strike against unity.

4.3. QUESTIONS (A) AND (B) REVISITED

So far we have not directly addressed the kinds of case invoked by proponents of QWQ. Are they grammatical? Are they equivalent to (4.1*)–(4.5*)? We think the answer to both questions is 'no'.

First, we suspect many of these cases *do* involve quotation marks tacitly. One way to show this is to establish that in many cases there are *elliptical* quotation marks. In these cases, there seems to be no quotation marks, but they are really there (for example, if the expression without quotation marks is of the wrong grammatical category, then that's a good reason for thinking there are elliptical quotation marks). So, although (4.10) turns out to be grammatical, (4.13) and (4.14) do not.[3]

*4.13. In the garden has three words.
*4.14. Abce is not a word of English.

---

[3] See Gomez-Torrente (2001: 137) for a related point.

A prepositional phrase can't be the subject of an English sentence and neither can nonsense. To the extent that you think such sentences are acceptable that must be because they are elliptic for their quotational variants (4.13.1) and (4.14.1):

4.13.1. 'In the garden' has three words.
4.14.1. 'Abce' is not a word of English.

If you want to deny these claims, then grammar as a subject matter we know will become either undoable or complex beyond belief.

Concerning those cases where there's no clear justification for attributing ellipsis, we suspect they can be easily explained away by appeal to familiar pragmatic mechanisms, such as conversational implicatures and the like. It is useful here to run the alleged evidence through the sort of test devised for a related purpose by Kripke (1977).

Consider a language English* like English in every respect with one (possible) exception: in English* it is impossible to quote without quotation marks (i.e. we assume that the cases appealed to by our opponents are ungrammatical in English*). Ask yourself: could a speaker assertively utter (4.10) and yet her audience understand her? Should we expect that English* speakers might occasionally omit (to use Saka's term) quotation marks? The answer, it seems to us, is trivially 'yes'. English* speakers could omit quotation marks whenever what is meant is obvious.

Take (4.10) as an example. It is clear to most audiences that the girl, i.e. Alice, isn't a noun (excluding situations that involve the introduction of strange sign systems in which people can be used to articulate linguistic units) and that the speaker is not in the business of thinking she is a noun. As a result, the speaker can get away with omitting the 'quote-unquote' part. The same goes for introductions, as in (4.3):

4.3. My name is Corey.

No one will think its speaker is claiming that the philosopher, Corey, is identical to his name. If English* speakers can omit quote marks and still convey what they mean, i.e. project the same readings and interpretations as we do in English, then the fact that we can omit quotation marks in English provides no evidence whatsoever that we are not ourselves English* speakers. We agree with Grice (1989: 47) that if you have two competing accounts of a linguistic phenomenon, one that requires stipulating a semantic ambiguity and one that only appeals to general pragmatic principles, Modified Ockam's Razor ('Don't multiply senses beyond necessity!') requires choosing the latter.

This is indeed the strategy employed by several of those who dismiss this kind of data. García-Carpintero, for example, says:

> we could easily explain what happens in the controversial cases by having recourse to the mechanism of conversational implicature. In this case, an utterance of what we intend to be <<'Barcelona' has nine letters>> without any conventional realization of quotation marks would count as an utterance saying that Barcelona—the city—has nine letters. Then we would explain how the audience gets the intended meaning through an easily derivable conversational implicature. ('He cannot be saying of Barcelona, the city, that it has nine letters'), for this is false, and he must know that it is false . . . therefore, he must be conversationally implicating, about the expression that he has used a token of, that it has nine letters. (García-Carpintero 1994: 263; for a closely related view that exploits the distinction between semantic reference and speaker reference, see Gomez-Torrente 2001: 130; see also Seymour 1996: 312)

On this view, (4.4.) is grammatically correct but false.

4.4. Donald is Davidson's name.

Nonetheless, someone can succeed in communicating something true about Davidson's name if he succeeds in conveying to his audience his intention to refer to it.

4.4. CONCLUSION AND OVERVIEW

We conclude that the data marshaled in support of the Quotation Without Quotation Marks thesis are not only irrelevant to traditional theories of quotation; there are plenty of strategies traditional theories can use to accommodate it. This will prove to be of great importance when we discuss Use Theories of Quotation in Chapter 8, and also underlies our positive view, presented in Chs. 11 and 12.

5

'Impure' Direct Quotes

Here are two interesting facts about direct quotations (and the quoted parts of mixed quotations): sometimes what's directly quoted is not a token of the original sentence uttered but rather its translation; furthermore, sometimes what's directly quoted improves on the original sentence uttered (omitted words filled in, grammatical infelicities repaired, repeated words eliminated, utterances of 'hmm', 'aahh', etc. eliminated). Sections 5.1–2 provide illustrations of what we have in mind.

5.1. TRANSLATED DIRECT QUOTATIONS

Consider the following passage from the *Guardian*, 10 Sept. 2005 (online):

Jacques Chirac left hospital yesterday, declaring himself 'in good shape', but aware that his week-long stay, for what doctors called 'a small vascular incident', had unleashed a fierce battle for his succession. The French president, 72, looked comfortable and said he felt 'very well'. He had been 'eager to leave'. The first thing he wanted to do now was 'to go and have lunch'. 'The president's health is consistent with what was in the hospital statements,' said one medical observer, Alain Ducardonnet, on television. 'The rumours about his health are over. He is clearly well.'

One thing for certain is that Chirac and Ducardonnet did not speak English. They spoke in French, as the French are wont to do. The quoted words in this passage, therefore, are translations of what they uttered. Translated direct quotations are not at all unusual. A casual perusal of any newspaper reveals their ubiquity.

In addition to journalists, philosophers also (as well as other scholars) do this sort of thing all the time. Here are familiar examples from Tsohatzidis (2005: 215):

3.21. Descartes said that man 'is a thinking substance'.
3.22. Frege said that predicate expressions 'are unsaturated'.

The sentences these philosophers tokened were not English, yet (3.21)–(3.22) are, just the same, true direct reports of what they uttered.

5.2. FIXER-UPPER QUOTATIONS

One fact universally known about President G. W. Bush is that he is less than adroit at producing grammatically well-formed sentences. This isn't just a point his opponents try to exploit, it is a view he himself often acknowledges in interviews and speeches. It is, indeed, a view of himself that he relishes with a sort of anti-intellectual pride. With this information as background, consider this transcript of an interview with Bush on the Fox News Channel (7 Sept. 2005):

Bush: I think that our FBI and Homeland Security people are working hand-in-glove to protect America on a daily basis. I was briefed on some of the particulars about the matter you just described. I can assure the American people that we're following every lead, that we're doing everything we can to keep us protected.

One works overseas by doing two things: one, committing our troops and intelligence services to the task, and also spreading freedom.

The way to defeat hatred and hopelessness in the long term is to lay foundations for peace by spreading freedom. So we've got a dual strategy that requires a lot of effort, a lot of sacrifice, but it's working.

These are representative segments of the transcript. Notice that, by and large, Bush is quoted as uttering complete, (practically) grammatical sentences. But, as a matter of fact, he uttered not a single complete grammatical sentence throughout his interview. Instead, his utterances were chock full of gaps, false starts, missing words, mistaken inflections, etc. In this regard, of course, he is indistinguishable from most other interviewees. The practice of fixing up recorded interview direct quotations is commonplace in the press. This is a point that Janet Malcolm (1990: 158–9) has made a great deal of:

Before the invention of the tape recorder, no quotation could be verbatim—what Boswell quotes Dr. Johnson as saying was obviously not precisely what Johnson said; we will never know what that was—and many journalists continue to work without benefit of this double-edged technological aid, doing their work of editing or paraphrasing on the spot, as they scribble in their notebooks . . . .The quotations in this book—and in my other journalistic writings—are not . . . identical to their speech counterparts.

Malcolm continues, and this might surprise readers, by pointing out:

> When we read a quotation in a newspaper story or in a text such as this one, we assume it to be a rendering of what the speaker actually—not probably—said. The idea of a reporter inventing rather than reporting speech is a repugnant, even sinister, one. . . . Fidelity to the subject's thought and to his characteristic way of expressing himself is the sine qua non of journalistic quotation—one under which all stylistic considerations are subsumed.

The fact is precise verbatim direct quotations are quite rare (cf. Clark and Gerrig 1990).

5.3. WHAT IS THE SIGNIFICANCE OF THESE DATA FOR A THEORY OF QUOTATION?

Our answer to the question of whether these data have any significance for a theory of quotation is 'None whatsoever'. It has no bearing on how we think about the semantics of quotation. Our argument is short and might even seem to some readers as dogmatic. The problem is that no argument has ever been advanced for an alternative view—all one finds in the literature on quotation is a denial of our claim that the data are irrelevant. And a denial does not an argument make.

There are two options we'll compare:

1. Translated and repaired direct and mixed quotations, as in (3.21)–(3.22) and (5.1)–(5.2), show something about what the quotations in these sentences quote, and hence, something about how quotation functions:

    5.1. Socrates said, 'The Unexamined Life is not worth living for a human'.

    5.2. Jacques Chirac left hospital yesterday, declaring himself 'in good shape', but aware that his week-long stay, for what doctors called 'a small vascular incident', had unleashed a fierce battle for his succession.

2. Translated and repaired direct and mixed quotations have no bearing whatsoever on the semantics for quotation: in (3.21)–(3.22) and (5.1)–(5.2), the direct and mixed quotations quote exactly what you would expect them to quote, i.e. ''in good shape'' quotes 'in good shape', ''is a thinking substance'' quotes 'is a thinking substance,' ''are unsaturated'' quotes 'are unsaturated', and so on.

5.3.1. In Defense of (2)

We take it to be almost *un*necessary to defend (2). In fact, it is hard to describe these data without assuming (2) is true. The natural way to describe the interesting feature of (3.21) is to say: (3.21) quotes the English 'is a thinking substance,' even though Descartes himself never uttered a single English expression. Descartes spoke and wrote exclusively in French and Latin; not in English. But then we might ask, how can (3.21) correctly quote English? Doesn't that require attributing to Descartes the use of English words? If it does, how can (3.21) be true? That's the puzzle. But notice this line of criticism presupposes that in (3.21) it is English words that are being quoted.

Here is how we understand these 'impure' cases: what these cases teach us is no more than something about the conditions under which a speaker can stand in a saying relation to a quoted item. Sentences (3.21)–(3.22) and (5.1)–(5.2) tell us that someone can stand in a saying relation to a quoted sentence (or sentence fragment) even though he never uttered a token of that sentence (or sentence fragment) but rather only a transla-tion of it in another language or an ill-formed version of it in the same language. In other words, there are data that should be accommodated by a theory of 'saying'; not by a (semantic) theory of quotation.

A theory of the saying relation will no doubt be exceedingly complex and the case of impure quotations is but one of a rather extensive set of puzzling cases that must be accommodated by a complete semantic theory for a natural language that includes not just the semantics of quotation but also the semantics of direct (and mixed) reporting. This point can be registered without actually having a theory. We have elsewhere (Cappelen and Lepore 1997*a*) conjectured that the saying relation isn't the kind of thing that lends itself to systematic theorizing—whether that view turns out to be correct or not we'll leave aside here (though we will take up the project of devising an account of direct and mixed quotations in Ch. 11).

5.3.2. What Does (1) Even Mean?[1]

Let's briefly consider option (1). We take it that no one in his right mind would hold either of (a), (b), or (c).

---

[1] Another view that has worked its way into print is that the quotation sentences like (5.1) can be true because in a context in which they are true, 'the extension of

a. In (5.1), the quotation ''the Unexamined Life is not worth living for a human'' refers to Greek words and not to English ones.

We know of no one who holds this view, so it's not an option worth considering.

b. In (5.1), the quotation marks are superfluous.

Were this true, it would turn direct reports into indirect ones. That flies in the face of all the data. No one skeptical of (2) has suggested that the solution is to obliterate the indirect/direct quotation distinction.

c. In (5.1), the quotations refer to some kind of conglomerate of English and Greek words.

Again, no one has ever suggested any such view, so we don't even know how to pursue it.

This leaves, as far as we can tell, but one option, i.e. that the quotes in (5.1) refer to what they seem to refer to, namely, 'the Unexamined Life is not worth living for a human'.

5.4. REPLIES FROM TSOHATZIDIS, SAKA, AND REIMER

Tsohatzidis (2005), Saka (2005), and Reimer (2005) have each strenuously objected to our seemingly obvious points, not so much with arguments for an alternative position, but rather by trying to show that our view leads to absurd results. Their efforts are based on misinterpretations of our position—to avoid such confusions we review some of their points here.

In Cappelen and Lepore (1997*b*), we said that the truth of translational direct and mixed quotations had something to do with the 'same-tokening relation' (that was our quasi-technical term for the 'say' of direct and mixed reports). We argued, as we did above, that it fails to show anything interesting about the semantics for quotation. In response, Tsohatzidis (2005: 218–19) writes:

the quotation would be in the intension of the quoted phrase' (Simchen 1999: 328). Wertheimer invokes the notion of 'trans-linguistic contents' instead (Wertheimer 1999: 515). It follows from this view that all synonymous expressions in such contexts are interchangeable inside these reports. That's just not so. We simply cannot report Tim's utterance of 'It was a vixen!' with 'Tim said, 'It was a female fox!' '

Let us assume, as C&L now propose, that sametokening is a relation that holds between two expressions when they are 'translations' of each other—that is, when their content is the same, even though their shapes may be wildly different. . . . interpreted as a way of recapturing the type/token distinction, it has obviously absurd implications (it implies, for example, that a token of the English word 'day' and a token of the French word 'jour' are tokens of the same word, simply because they happen to have the same content, or that a token of the word 'pianoforte' and a token of the word 'fortepiano' are tokens of the same word, simply because they both happen to refer to the same musical instrument).

Tsohatzidis adds:

The real problem with the new account is that, by proposing an understanding of sametokening based on the notion of translation—and so, exclusively on content preservation, rather than on shape-preservation—the new account makes the sametokening relation indistinguishable from the samesaying relation, contrary to what C&L's general views about quotation explicitly require.

Following up on this line of argument, Saka (2005: 211) says:

. . . their position allows same-tokening to be coextensive with, or even broader than, same-saying: indirect discourse reports would absurdly entail the corresponding direct discourse.

Reimer (2005: 185) says:

. . . Cappelen and Lepore (1998) suggest that the problem can be solved by adopting a notions of "same-tokening" flexible enough to allow words to same-token different (though appropriately related) words. My suspicion is that this sort of move has the effect of artificially insulating the theory against counter-examples.

For related comments, see also Tsohatzidis (1998), Elugardo (1999), and Stainton (1999).

5.5. OUR REPLY

We suspect that all of these criticisms are based on reading into our position a view that we never advocated: 'same-tokening,' as we noted above, is a quasi-technical word we coined for the 'say' of a direct and mixed quotation. We regret the use of this expression, but not the idea we intended it to encode. Our critics seem to assume that we hold the following thesis:

Let S_e be an English sentence and S_f a sentence or fragment of a sentence in another language F. Suppose S_e translates S_f. Suppose also that A uttered S_f speaking language F. That's sufficient for a direct and mixed report with S_e filling the quotes to be true.

Put more simply, our critics attribute to us the view that it is a sufficient condition on a true direct report that the reportee uttered a sentence or sentence fragment that can be translated into the sentence or sentence fragment quoted in the complement of the direct or mixed report. We don't suggest (and never have suggested) any such sufficient condition. We simply observe that in some of these cases we have the intuition that a direct or mixed report is true (despite the quoted material being, for example, translated). That this is so can't be because these are cases where what's quoted aren't the words blatantly quoted (see the arguments above). So it has *something* to do with the saying relation, and not with quotation *per se* (at least if you want to preserve the intuitions that these are true reports, a goal we share with our critics). Exactly what it has to do with that saying relation, we're not quite sure. These are tricky issues. But one thing is for sure—these data have nothing whatsoever to do with quotation—a topic we do have views about (see Gomez-Torrente 2005: 136).[2]

You might think it's cheating for us not to give an account of the saying relation. You might think it would be desirable if we were able to specify the conditions under which a subject stands in the saying relation to a quoted item. We agree it would be exceedingly interesting and impressive and lovely were someone to devise such a theory. We are not optimistic that anyone ever will, and we can only report that we ourselves have been unable to do so. The point we make here is simply that we can do the semantics for quotation without any such theory.

---

[2] Moreover, we never meant to present a sufficient condition for when two tokens are of the same expression type. That we were so interpreted must be the result of a somewhat confusing terminology we were using at the time (e.g. using 'same-tokening' made it sound like we were trying to give a theory of when tokens are of the same expression type—that's not the role that this term played in Cappelen and Lepore (1997*b*): it was a stand-in for the 'said' of direct reports, much as 'same-saying' was a stand-in for Davidson (1968) for the 'said' of indirect reports). We did, however, suggest a methodological principle that we still embrace: there should be no a priori constraint on how to understand the saying relation. We have argued elsewhere (see Cappelen and Lepore 1997*a*: 2004) that there's a philosophical tradition that tends to place constraints on what can same-say (or same-token, for that matter) what. All our work is fundamentally opposed to that tradition.

5.6. CONCLUSION AND OVERVIEW

We conclude that 'impure quotes' don't pose a challenge to a theory of quotation, though do present a challenge for a theory of the *saying relation*. This will prove to be significant in the next chapter, where we discuss the nature of mixed quotation. In sect. 6.3, where we appeal to the non-cancelability of mixed quotation, issues about 'impure quotes' will come up again.

6

Is Mixed Quotation Semantically Redundant?

Some philosophers (including earlier time-slices of Cappelen and Lepore) think that in mixed quotation, as in (1.10), the quoted words are simultaneously used and mentioned (i.e. there's simultaneous direct and indirect quotation going on):

1.10. Quine said that quotation 'has a certain anomalous feature'.

For these authors, it's apparent that (1.10) says both what Quine said and some of the expressions he used in saying it.

The sole topic of this chapter is to explore one small aspect of mixed quotation, namely, whether it is a genuinely semantic phenomenon.[1] We will argue against a Redundancy View (RV) of mixed quotation, according to which:

> **RV:** The quotation marks in mixed quotations are semantically superfluous.

RV says that the semantic content of (1.10) is preserved and can indeed be isolated simply by removing its quotation marks. So understood, the quotation marks in (1.10) have no semantic role whatsoever. This, of course, doesn't mean that they have *no* role, though proponents of RV disagree about what it is. We will outline several options below.

RV has an important corollary in CRV:

> **CRV:** The semantic content of a mixed report is identical to the semantic content of the corresponding direct report (i.e. one in which its complement clause has no quotation marks).

---

[1] The question of whether mixed quotes are legitimate cases where the quoted words are used and mentioned we won't take up until Ch. 11—where we'll conclude, *contra* everyone else who has ever written on the topic from Davidson onward, including a past time-slice of ourselves, that they are not used at all.

According to CRV, the indirect report made by a mixed quotation can be located by removing its quotation marks. The indirect report made by (1.10), then, is (1.9):

1.9. Quine said that quotation has a certain anomalous feature.

CRV follows from RV, so if the former is false, so is the latter.

An alternative to the RV is the Semantic View (SV) of mixed quotation:

> **SV**: The semantic contribution of quotation marks in mixed quotation is the same as in pure and direct quotation.[2]

SV requires that we devise a semantic theory for quotation marks to account for their occurrence in mixed quotation: either this semantics somehow manages to let the words inside mixed quotation be used and mentioned simultaneously (that might seem intuitive) or just mentioned. (Again, in Ch. 11, we defend the latter view.) The goal of this chapter is not to defend SV—it is only to present evidence against both RV and CRV.

6.1. MORE ON RV

RV is defended by, among others, Recanati (2001) (who bases his work on Clark and Gerrig 1990), Stainton (1999), Reimer (though not fully endorsed) (2005), Saka (2005), García-Carpintero (2005: 102–3) and Wertheimer (1999). Recanati (2001: 660) writes that within his framework:

it is simply not true that the proposition expressed by the complement sentence in [1.10] is 'about words', as Cappelen and Lepore claim (without argument). [. . .] *On the present proposal, however, the proposition expressed by the complement sentence is the same with or without the quotation marks, and it is not about words.* (our emphasis)

When, for example, Davidson utters (1.10), according to Recanati, his audience must recognize that Davidson intends to let them know that Quine used the words 'has a certain anomalous feature'. This information, according to Recanati, is communicated via various pragmatic

---

[2] There are of course other alternatives to RV, e.g. that quotation marks are semantically ambiguous in various ways.

mechanisms and not on the basis of the semantics of (1.10) alone. He writes (2001: 667):

The last mentioned aspect of the interpretation [i.e. *that Davidson wanted to communicate that Quine used the words 'has a certain anomalous feature'*] is clearly pragmatic [. . .]. It is a matter of *identifying the point of the demonstration*. If this is right, then the ascription of the quoted words to the person whose speech or thought is reported is not even a conventional implicature. It belongs to the most pragmatic layer of interpretation, where one tries to *make sense of the speaker's act of demonstration in the broader context in which it takes place*. This is not 'interpretation' in the narrowly linguistic sense.

Stainton (1999: 273–4), another proponent of RV, concurs:

A speaker could report parts of Alice's conversation in a squeaky voice, or with a French accent, or with a stutter, or using great volume. In none of these cases would the speech reporter *say, assert, or state* that Alice spoke in these various ways. [. . .] In these cases, the truth conditions of the speech report are exhausted by the meaning of the words, and how the words are put together; *as far as truth conditions are concerned, the tone, volume, accent etc. add nothing whatever. Ditto, say I, for the quotation marks in mixed quotation.* In which case, (6) [Alice said that quotation 'is difficult to understand'] isn't false where Alice actually speaks the words 'is tough to understand'. It may, of course, be infelicitous and misleading.   (our emphasis)

In a similar vein, Saka (2005) claims that a mixed quotation is 'assertorically equivalent' to the indirect report that results from removing the quotation marks.

All these writers explicitly endorse CRV and vary somewhat in their formulation of RV.

6.2. ARGUMENTS IN FAVOR OF THE SEMANTIC ACCOUNT OF MIXED QUOTATION

The remainder of this chapter is devoted to refuting RV and CRV. We will marshal four arguments.

6.2.1. Argument 1 Against RV: Simple Intuitions

As a report of Quine's utterance of (6.1), most speakers would say (1.10) is false, and that (6.2) is compatible with it.

6.1. Quotation has some unusual properties.

6.2. Quine said that quotation 'has an unusual property'.

1.10. Quine said that quotation 'has a certain anomalous feature'.

Still we can agree that both (1.9) and (6.3) are correct indirect reports of Quine's utterance of (6.1):[3]

1.9. Quine said that quotation has a certain anomalous feature.

6.3. Quine said that quotation has an unusual property.

One might disagree about how much weight we should confer on such intuitions (and we have doubts ourselves (Cappelen and Lepore 2004)), but these intuitions are not irrelevant: they certainly must be accommodated and they provide at least a *prima facie* case against RV and CRV. For an elaboration of just this point, see Reimer (2005).

6.2.2. Argument 2 Against RV: Three Counter-Examples

According to RV, quotation marks in mixed quotations are superfluous; so we can remove them without a change in meaning. On this account, what the reported speaker said is what's expressed by the complement clause with its quotation marks removed. Here are several cases that provide evidence against this view:

Case 1: Indexicals in Mixed Quotation

Recall once again this example of a mixed quotation from Cappelen and Lepore (1997*b*: 429):

> Mr. Greenspan said he agreed with Labor Secretary R. B. Reich 'on quite a lot of things'. Their accord on this issue, he said, has proved 'quite a surprise to both of us.'

As we pointed out in Ch. 1, the occurrence of 'us' in the last sentence of this passage does not refer to the journalist and his audience. Yet were the quotation marks in this sentence semantically superfluous (as they are according to CRV theorists), then the occurrence of 'us' should be read as spoken by the journalist (i.e. by the reporter), making reference to him and his intended audience.

---

[3] For our view of the flexibility of indirect reports, see Cappelen and Lepore (1998; 2004).

The following two examples from Cumming (2005: 78) make our point even clearer:

(C1) Bush also said his administration would 'achieve our objectives' in Iraq.

(C2) He now plans to make a new, more powerful absinthe that he says will have 'a more elegant, refined taste than the one I'm making now'.

Remember that, according to Recanati (2001: 660), 'the proposition expressed by the complement sentence is the same with or without the quotation marks'. And according to Stainton, 'as far as truth conditions are concerned, the [quotation marks in mixed quotation] add nothing whatever'. But, go ahead and try to remove them! What results are (C1*) and (C2*):

(C1*) Bush also said his administration would achieve our objectives in Iraq.

(C2*) He now plans to make a new, more powerful absinthe that he says will have a more elegant, refined taste than the one I'm making now.

These are obviously mistaken renderings of (C1) and (C2). This is powerful evidence that quotation marks in mixed quotes make a semantic difference.

Recanati disagrees. Below we'll present and evaluate his responses.

Case 2: Quotation of Nonsense

Consider (6.4) (from Cappelen and Lepore 1997*b*) and (6.5) as examples:

6.4. Nicola said that Alice is a 'philtosopher'.
6.5. Robert claims Mary to be 'the loesser of two evils'.

Try removing the quotation marks, say, from (6.4) (which should provide the semantic content, according to RV) results in (6.6):

6.6*. Nicola said that Alice is a philtosopher.

The speakers of (6.4) and (6.5) might not know what 'philtosopher' means or might be indicating that Robert misspoke with his use of 'loesser'; these might not be words in his language. They might be gibberish. He may not be sure and that may explain why he mixed quoted. Example (6.6) doesn't capture the content of (6.4).

Case 3: Quotation of Foreign Expressions

Consider (6.7) or (6.8):

6.7. Descartes said that he thinks, 'ergo sum'.
6.8. Galileo said that the Earth 'si muove'.

These are perfectly normal examples where the quotation part of the mixed quotation sentence is in a foreign language. Disquoting these quotes in (6.7) or (6.8) results in a gibberish hybrid from two languages, and so they cannot be what these sentences express.

6.2.2.1. Recanati's Responses to Argument 2

Recanati responds to these kinds of case as objections to RV and CRV. His replies are closely related in that they all invoke the same mechanism to accommodate the seemingly controverting data within his account. We present his discussion and then our replies.

6.2.2.1.1. Recanati on Indexicals in Mixed Quotation: Context Shift
Recanati, much to his credit, tackles (some of) the data presented, but fails to recognize their devastating implications for his own view. His response (see Recanati 2001: 674-80) is twofold: he holds that in alleged cases of context shifting there is a semantic effect (on what he calls c-content), i.e. the quotation influences semantic content, but that the effect is not 'a direct semantic effect'. It is only *indirect* via a *pre-semantic* effect. Here's Recanati's view in summary (what follows paraphrases Recanati *ibid.*): The notion of a pre-semantic process is from Kaplan (1989: 559), who says: 'Given an utterance, semantics cannot tell us what expression was uttered or what language it was uttered in. This is a pre-semantic task.' Another example of a pre-semantic task is disambiguation. If a word has more than one meaning, semantics won't tell you which one is intended on a particular occasion. Of course, pre-semantic processes affect semantic content, but only 'indirectly'. About language selection, Recanati (2001: 676) writes, 'the process of semantic composition which outputs the c-content [what we call 'semantic content'] takes the meaning of the constituent words as input, and the meaning of the constituent words itself depends upon the language(s) to which the words in question are taken to belong'. In other words, even though language selection influences semantic content, it does so only indirectly by determining the input to the

semantic machinery that churns out semantic content: 'That process of input-determination is, by definition, pre-semantic' (*ibid.*).

Sense selection (i.e. the choice faced with ambiguity) has the same kind of pre-semantic, hence 'indirect', effect on semantic content. In sum: language and sense selection are paradigm pre-semantic processes.

Why does any of this concern the interpretation of indexicals inside mixed quotations like (C1) and (C2)? Faced with such counter-examples (he specifically discusses our Greenspan mixed quote), Recanati concurs that quotation marks do affect semantic content, but only *indirectly*. They affect pre-semantic processes and thereby have only an indirect effect on semantic content. In this respect, he is claiming that the phenomena are like language and sense selection. The quotation marks (in effect, the accompanying demonstration[4]) tell us *which context we should consider those words as uttered in*. The quotation marks (and the accompanying demonstration) tell us that the quoted words should be interpreted as being uttered by the person being reported, and not by the context of the person uttering the indirect report. In (C1), the quotation serves the pre-semantic function of telling us that the quoted words should be interpreted as uttered by Bush, and not by whoever happens to utter (C1):

(C1) Bush also said his administration would 'achieve our objectives' in Iraq.

In (C2), the quotation serves the pre-semantic function of telling us that the quoted words should be interpreted as uttered by the reported individual at the time of her original utterance and not by whoever happens to utter (C2) and relative to whenever she happens to utter it:

(C2) He now plans to make a new, more powerful absinthe that he says will have 'a more elegant, refined taste than the one I'm making now.'

In sum: Recanati concludes that indexicals inside mixed quotation do have semantic impact, but he insists that this impact is pre-semantic, and hence, only indirect.

6.2.2.1.2. Recanati on Mixed-Quoted Nonsense: Language Shift
In response to the fact that we can mixed quote nonsense, Recanati makes a similar move. Discussing (6.4),

---

[4] Quotation marks for Recanati do nothing but indicate the speaker's demonstrative intentions.

6.4. Nicola said that Alice is a 'philtosopher'.

he says (*ibid.*), 'The expression in quotation is understood as belonging to someone's idiolect (Paul's, James's or Nicola's) in contrast to the rest of the sentence. As a result that expression is given a special meaning, which determines a special content.' In such cases 'the expression within the quotation marks is not used with its standard meaning, but with the meaning it has for *the person whose use is being echoically simulated*' (*ibid.* 674; our emphasis). The quotation marks thereby affect 'a language shift' (*ibid.*). We are using the quoted words with the meaning they have in the quoted person's idiolect (*ibid.*).[5]

This does not mean that the quotations function semantically, according to Recanati. These are pre-semantic processes. They 'affect the content of the utterance, by determining the language which is relevant to the interpretation of the expression in quotes' (*ibid.* 676). Semantic content is affected, but, again, only indirectly 'through determination of the input to the semantic process which outputs the c-content. That process of input-determination is, by definition, pre-semantic' (*ibid.*).

6.2.2.2. *Response to Recanati's Account of Indexicals and Nonsense in Mixed Quotation*

Our response to Recanati's account of indexicals and nonsense in mixed quotation is threefold: we first show why his theory fails to account for the data, and then why, even if it did, it would undermine his defense of RV and CRV. And finally, we point out disanalogies between language selection and context shifting.

First Part of Our Reply to Recanati: His View Fails to Account for the Data

It is an essential requirement on Recanati's account of mixed quoted indexicals and nonsense that the report picks out (or somehow determines) a context of utterance for the reported utterance; in Recanati's terminology that it 'echoes' a speaker. If a mixed quote didn't, in any way, echo some speaker or other, then the theory fails: we would not know which context to interpret the indexicals 'as uttered in', and we would not know which language to shift to (in the case of nonsense quotes). In other words: the maneuvers described above require that

---

[5] It is not obvious to us how Recanati can use this strategy to account for mixed quotations involving languages other than the language used outside the quotes. In these cases, there's no language to switch to, since no one speaks a language that combines, say, English and French. We won't pursue this objection here.

there be someone whose context we can shift to (with mixed quoted indexicals) and someone whose language we shift to (with mixed quoted nonsense). It is, however, easy to devise cases where there is no one to echo, and hence, no context to shift to (whether it be context shift or language shift). Consider (6.9)–(6.11):

> 6.9. No one said that Alice was a 'philtosopher'.
> 6.10. Someone said that Alice was a 'philtosopher'.
> 6.11. No one said that the absinthe 'is better than the one I'm making now.'

These cases establish that what goes on in the other cases isn't a shift in context or language from the speaker to *someone else's language or context,* since there is *no context* to shift to and *no one* to echo.

These are not the only cases where Recanati's theory encounters difficulties. Consider the following dialogue:

> S: Alice said that Nicola is a 'philtosopher'.
> R: Ted said that too.

How are we to interpret R's utterance, according to Recanti? Note that it is possible Ted used 'philtosopher' to mean something other than what Alice used it to mean. So, switching to Alice's context and interpreting 'philtosopher' to mean whatever she meant by it (in the relevant context of utterance) need not get you what Ted said. But our intuition, anyway, is that this utterance of 'Ted said that too' would be true under those circumstances.

Second Part of Our Reply to Recanati: Pre-semantic = Semantic

In effect, Recanati acknowledges that the quotation marks in mixed quotation have a semantic effect, and he tries to salvage his non-semantic account by calling the effect 'pre-semantic'. Re-labeling a phenomenon, however, won't change the facts, and the facts are these:

> **F1:** The behavior of indexicals establishes that the quotation marks in mixed quotation determine semantic content (what Recanati calls c-content).

> **F2:** Remove the quotation marks, and you change the semantic content. What you get is a proposition that is not, at any level of analysis, expressed by any utterance of, for example, (C1) and (C2). In other words, Recanati's claim that 'the proposition expressed by the complement sentence is the same with or without the quotation marks' (Recanati 2001: 660) is simply *not* true.

F3: The semantic effect of the quotation marks is not determined by speaker intentions (demonstrative or otherwise). A speaker can have whatever intentions she wants, but these do not alter the fact that indexicals inside mixed quotation cannot be read as spoken by the reporter (the person uttering the sentence with mixed quotation). In other words, Recanati's claim that quotation 'belongs to the most pragmatic layer of interpretation, where one tries to *make sense of the speaker's act of demonstration in the broader context in which it takes place*' (*ibid.* 667) is also *not* true.

What matters is not the terminology we use; it doesn't matter whether we call the effect of mixed quotation *semantic, pre-semantic, or schemantic*. What matters, and what concerns us in this chapter, is whether RV and CRV are true. What should be clear is that (F1)–(F3) suffice to undermine any non-semantic account of mixed quotation. So, if we put aside the terminological issues, Recanati's account, by virtue of endorsing (F1)–(F3), fails to support RV and CRV.

Third Part of Our Reply to Recanati: Indexicals in Mixed Quotation are not Analogous to Language Selection

Re-labeling aside, the analogy between context shifting for indexicals and language/sense selection is not a good one. In the case of language selection, speaker intentions have the final word. Take an utterance of 'MIA LOVES FRED.' If we tell you it was uttered as an English sentence, it means one thing (*namely, that Mia loves Fred*). If we tell you it was uttered as a Norwegian sentence, it means something else (*namely that Mia is being promised peace*). *We* (i.e. Cappelen and Lepore) get to choose which language the utterance is in. It is, however, *not* up to Tom how indexicals inside the quotation marks get interpreted. He *cannot*, for example, choose to have them interpreted relative to his own context. In this regard, it surely looks as if, to the extent that you believe that indexicals have a semantic interpretation inside mixed quotations, this determination is rule-like and semantic.[6]

We turn to a third argument against RV and its corollary CRV.

---

[6] For an alternative criticism of Recanati on indexicals inside mixed quotation, cf. Benbaji (2005: 43 ff.). For our evaluation of the data, see Ch. 11.

6.2.3. Argument 3: Argument from Non-Cancelability

We're assuming that if a component of the content expressed by a sentence S is not cancelable, we have good reason to believe it is part of the semantic content of S. That ''has an anomalous feature'' is not cancelable in (1.10) can be shown using both Grice's cancelability tests. Grice (1989: 44) distinguishes between *explicit* and *contextual* cancelability; he writes:

a putative conversational implicature that *p* is explicitly cancelable if, to the form of words the utterance of which putatively implicates that *p*, it is admissible to add *but not p*, or *I do not mean to imply that p*, and it is contextually cancelable if one can find situations in which the utterance of the form of words would simply not carry the implicature.

That 'has an anomalous feature' being quoted is not explicitly cancelable is evidenced by its being very hard to conjure up a false utterance of (6.12):

6.12. Quine said that quotation 'has an anomalous feature,' but 'has an anomalous feature' has not been quoted.

This shows that the expression being quoted in (1.10) is *not* cancelable. So, we have evidence that the quotation ''has an anomalous feature'' is part of the semantic content of (1.10).

6.2.3.1. Reimer on the Argument from Non-Cancelability

Reimer (2005: 175) responds to the non-cancelability argument; she says:

[a proponent of RV]...might point out that semantic theories of mixed quotation have counter-intuitive consequences when applied to speech reports involving translation. Consider the following mixed quotations (all of which are from Tsohatzidis, 1998):

3.21 Descartes said that man 'is a thinking substance'.
3.22 Frege said that predicate expressions 'are unsaturated'.
6.13 Socrates said that an unexamined life 'is not worth living for a human'.

As Reimer points out, it seems intuitive to say that all of (3.21)–(3.22) and (6.13) are true, despite the fact that 'neither Descartes, Frege, nor Socrates wrote what they 'said' in English' (Reimer, *ibid.*). From this,

Reimer concludes that the cancellation test might turn against those who deny RV.[7] She says (*ibid.*):

The cancellability test can seemingly be passed after all, as there would be nothing amiss with an utterance of [(6.14)]:

> 6.14 Descartes said that man "is a thinking substance," but he didn't use those very words, as he wrote only in French and Latin.

So, semantic accounts of mixed quotation—at least the version proposed by Cappelen and Lepore (1997)—appear to have counter-intuitive results . . .

The counter-intuitive result is that we predict non-cancelability where there's evidence of cancelability. In other words, what we take to be support for our objection to RV is, according to Reimer, potentially an objection to our own position.

Without rehearsing the arguments from Ch. 5, it should be obvious how to apply the conclusions from that chapter here: translational mixed-quotes don't show that words quoted are not quoted. The words 'is a thinking substance' are quoted in (6.14). That, we take it, is undisputed (no one, as we pointed out in the previous chapter, thinks it is the French or Latin words that are being quoted). What these examples show is that the truth of (3.21) is compatible with Descartes' not writing or speaking English. That, we argued, showed us something interesting about the saying relation (about what it takes for a subject to stand in the saying relation to a quoted item).

Remember, the kind of data Reimer appeals to is this: the speaker of e.g. (3.21) says something that can be true if Descartes wrote *that man is a thinking substance* and did it using words translatable into English as 'is a thinking substance'. That's of course just a first stab at a paraphrase (and we in no way intend it as a final theoretic account). But what's important is this: there's no way to explain what is going on in these cases without quoting 'is a thinking substance.' Sentence (3.21) says something about the relationship between what Descartes wrote and the words 'is a thinking substance.'[8] Maybe the relationship is literal translation; we won't take a stand on that here, but what is clear is that

---

[7] We should point out that Reimer's paper takes the form of *exploring* a number of arguments in connection with mixed quotation, and does not take a dogmatic stand on the ultimate soundness of these arguments. In particular, she does not ultimately endorse this objection to the cancelability argument.

[8] See Gomez-Torrente (2005: 135–6) for a related point.

the quotation of the expression 'is a thinking substance' in (3.21) is *in*eliminable.

Some of the confusion that arises from these cases might have to do with the issue of how we are to phrase the conjunct that's doing the cancellation. Reimer (2005) discusses a proposal from Cappelen (personal communication) that in order to test whether the mixed quote is cancelable, we try our intuitions on sentences like: "'Quine said that quotation 'has a certain anomalous feature,' but those were not the words he used'" (*ibid.* 178). Reimer points out that if this is our test case, it is not at all clear that we can't cancel. She says:

> You are under the impression that Quine wrote only in German and have just been asked about his views on quotation. So you utter [(1.10)] [= *Quine said that quotation 'has a certain anomalous feature.'*] but then add, 'he didn't use those words though; I think he said it in German.' (*ibid.* 179) . . . .
>
> The data here suggest that propositions to the effect that the agent used the quoted words can indeed be canceled. But if so, those propositions cannot (*pace* Cappelen) be part of the mixed quotation sentence's 'compositionally determined truth conditional meaning.' Any intuition to the effect that they are is arguably the result of a myopic view of the linguistic data . . . (*ibid.* 180)

First note that the suggestion from Cappelen (that Reimer discusses) uses the term 'use those words' in the second conjunct (the cancelling conjunct). That's not the kind of cancellation opponents of RV should be focused on. What a proponent of non-cancelability should focus on is whether *the quoting of the words* is cancelable (remember the goal here is to refute RV). Loosely speaking, we're interested in whether the reference to those words can be cancelled.[9] As we pointed out in Ch. 5, it's not at all clear what relationship must hold between a speaker and a sequence of quoted words for that speaker to have said those words. We don't take a stand on that issue here. In particular, we're not committed to the view that the speaker must have 'used those words' (whatever that turns out to mean).

It's interesting to note that Reimer's imagined cancellation presupposes that the words 'has a certain anomalous feature' have been referred to in (1.10). The cancellation takes the form of uttering: 'He didn't use those words though; I think he said it in German' as a second conjunct.

---

[9] One reservation about this formulation: we're not sure whether 'refer' will turn out to be the right term at the end of the day; however, used loosely and non-theoretically, it's perfectly fine.

The expression 'those words' used in the alleged cancellation will naturally be read as referring to the words quoted by the quotation marks in the first conjunct of (1.10). That this is a natural reading of Reimer's example shows that, contrary to Reimer's reading of it, it provides evidence against cancelability (when that is properly understood).

6.4. CONCLUSION

We conclude, then, that RV and CRV are both false. Therefore, it follows that we must assign a semantic function to quotation marks within mixed quotation. How to achieve this end within a viable semantic theory for quotation is the topic of Ch. 11.

7
Quotation and Context Sensitivity

Can one and the same quotation be used on different occasions to quote distinct objects? The view that it can is taken for granted throughout much of the literature (e.g. Goddard and Routley 1966; Christensen 1967; Davidson 1979; Goldstein 1984; Jorgensen, Miller, and Sperber 1984; Atlas 1989; Clark and Gerrig 1990; Washington 1992; García-Carpintero 1994, 2004, 2005; Reimer 1996; Saka 1998). Here, as a reminder from Ch. 3, are examples of the sort of data marshaled in support of this view.

The quotation expression ' 'gone' ' can quote any of the following:

7.1. The expression (' 'gone' is dissyllabic');
7.2. Different types instantiated by the tokens (' '*gone*' is cursive');
7.3. Different types somehow related to the token (say, the graphic version of the uttered quoted material, or the spoken version of the inscribed quoted material, as in ' 'gone' sounds nice');
7.4. Different tokens somehow related to the quoted token ('What was the part of the title of the movie which, by falling down, caused the killing?—'gone' was');
7.5. The quoted token itself ('At least one of these words is heavier than 'gone' ' which you should imagine written in big wooden letters). (García-Carpintero 1994: 261.)

García-Carpintero also says:

7.6. There are contexts in which the quotations '*Madrid*' and 'Madrid' would have the same content, but there are easily conceivable contexts in which they would have different contents . . . (ibid. 260; cf. also García-Carpintero 2005: 97)

On the basis of these and similar examples (see Ch. 3), many theorists infer the thesis of Quotation Context Sensitivity (QCS):[1]

---

[1] QCS is endorsed by Davidson (1979) (see Ch. 10) inasmuch as his theory explicates quotation by locating a demonstrative element in it. Therefore, anyone who elaborates on

QCS: Let S be a sentence with a quotation Q.[2] Two utterances, u
and u′, of S can express different propositions because Q in u and
in u′ quotes different items.

One goal in this chapter is to refute any semantic interpretation of
QCS and also to show that even a pragmatic construal of the data
encounters problems. In sect. 7.1 we present four arguments against a
semantic construal of QCS. These arguments are not intended to deny
that data like (7.1)–(7.7) support QCS; we intend only to deny that
they should be explained by a semantic theory. In sect. 7.2 we quickly
present some pragmatic options for explaining these data in support
of QCS and then argue that some of these variability data resist even
pragmatic explanation. That result leaves us with an explanatory gap
that we will not be able to fill until Ch. 12. There we argue that a
proper understanding of the relevant data requires an acknowledgment
of something hitherto overlooked—namely, that distinct sentences
with distinct quotation expressions have been conflated in the service
of QCS.

7.1. WHAT'S WRONG WITH A SEMANTIC EXPLANATION OF QCS?

Is the variability data about quotational usage best explained by positing
(semantic) context sensitivity (or ambiguity/indeterminacy[3]) for quotation expressions? Were it so, quotation expressions would be behaving
semantically like indexical or demonstrative expressions, for example,
like 'I', 'now', and 'that', in that their semantic values would vary
between contexts of utterance. Two utterances of the same sentence
can disagree in truth-value because the semantic value of its quotation
expression changes across contexts of use. We have four objections to
this view, outlined in sects. 7.1.1–7.1.4 below.

Davidson's theory, such as Bennett (1988), García-Carpintero (1994), Reimer (1996),
and earlier time-slices of ourselves (1997*b*), endorses a semantic interpretation of the
data like (7.1)–(7.6) in support of QCS (though not all of Davidson's proponents use it
explicitly to explain these data).

   [2] Where S contains no context-sensitive expressions other than possibly Q.

   [3] We concentrate on the context sensitivity proposal in what follows, but what we say
obviously extends to any sort of semantic construal of QCS, including ambiguity and/or
indeterminacy.

7.1.1. Disquotation

The first worry with a semantic explanation of QCS is that it would block an explanation of the most intriguing (and surprisingly the most ignored) aspect of quotation: namely, what we called in Ch. 3 its (strong) disquotational nature, as exemplified in QS and SDS:

  (QS) ''e'' quotes 'e'.
  (SDS) Only ''e'' quotes 'e'.

(where 'e' is replaceable by any quotable item whatsoever in all of its occurrences). According to QS, disquoting a quotation expression thereby automatically retrieves whatever item it quotes. Solely by virtue of their linguistic properties, disquotational quotation sentences like (7.7) are rendered true.

7.7. ''Quine'' quotes 'Quine'.

One serious problem with a semantic construal of the data in support of QCS is that it cannot guarantee the truth of (dis)quotational sentences like (7.7).

First of all, a quotation sentence, *qua* sentence, doesn't have a truth-value (any more than an indexical sentence like 'I'm here now' does). According to a (semantic) context-sensitive treatment of quotation, sentences with quotation expressions only express propositions and only have truth conditions relative to (or in) contexts of utterance. So, if quotation expressions were (semantically) context-sensitive, (7.7) should be on par with (7.8):

7.8. 'that' demonstrates that.

But (7.8) is clearly defective in a way that (7.7) is not. Not including a reference to the utterance of 'that' in (7.8) renders it bizarre; no such bizarreness reaction is triggered by (7.7).

Furthermore, consider, for example, a particular utterance u of (7.7), where the first quotation expression we'll call Q1 and its second Q2. Call the object quoted by u of Q2, t2. Since what u of Q1 quotes depends on speaker intentions (or contextual salience), all the speaker of (7.7) would have to do to make (7.7) false would be to intend for u of Q1 to quote something other than t2 (or render something other than t2 contextually salient). A semantic construal of QCS allows for this, and hence, makes it easy to falsify both QS and SDS. But to be told we're not guaranteed of the truth of a quotation sentence like (7.7), as a matter of meaning alone,[4] will surprise most competent speakers.[5]

7.1.2. Proximity

In Ch. 2, we connected QS and SDS to the somewhat metaphorical idea of *proximity*. We presented several ways of cashing out this idea. No matter how this idea is ultimately developed, it is hard, if not impossible, to see how a semantic construal of QCS can respect it. As the theory is presented by its proponents, it is no constraint whatsoever on what can be quoted that it satisfy any of the different ways in which the proximity constraint can be spelled out. This is most obvious if we treat proximity as a form of containment (which we'll ultimately settle on in Ch. 11). If what a quotation expression quotes depends on the speaker's intentions in the way García-Carpintero suggests, then the containment idea is impossible to preserve. Consider, for example, (7.4) (one of García-Carpintero's examples of how speakers' intentions can determine what a quotation quotes):

> 7.4. Different tokens somehow related to the quoted token ('What was the part of the title of the movie which, by falling down, caused the killing? — 'gone' was').

Clearly, a piece of a movie poster can't be part of the linguistic expression ''gone'' (if it were, forget about uttering or writing it down).[6] In Ch. 3, we considered three other ways of cashing out Proximity:

> 1. . . . a quotation somehow pictures what it is about (Davidson 1979: 82).

---

[4] Indexical sentences can, of course, be knowable *a priori*, such as 'I'm here now'. Its *a priori* status is inferred from the character of its indexical expressions. The proposal we are now considering about the context sensitivity of quotation does not ascribe characters that would secure this kind of apriority to (7.7) or SDS. To see why, note that the view we are considering would allow both ''Madrid' = 'Madrid'' and '''Madrid'' = ''Madrid''' to be false. That said, we want to be clear that we don't mean to rule out the *in principle* possibility that context-sensitive terms have characters that can underwrite some apriorities. Thanks to John Hawthorne for forcing us to worry about this point.

[5] The weight you should place on this intuition will of course depend, in large part, on your view of context sensitivity and how transparent you should expect the phenomenon to be for speakers. We are among those who are highly skeptical of views that postulate *surprising* context sensitivity (Cappelen and Lepore 2004: 112–13) — the claim that there can be a false utterance of (7.7) is one of those.

[6] We also mentioned in Ch. 3 that others have spelled out the proximity idea without appeal to containment. As far as we can tell, all these alternatives are also incompatible with a semantic construal of QCS. We provide one additional illustration of this in Ch. 8.

2. A quotation is . . . a *hieroglyph* . . . [that] designates its object . . . by picturing it (Quine 1940: 26).
3. . . . we can go from knowing the quotation of any expression to knowing the expression itself (Saka 1998: 116).

It is hard to see how a semantic construal of QCS can satisfy any of these. There is no requirement built in that secures any kind of picturing or hieroglyphic relationship between the quotation and its semantic value. Given that the speaker's intention (together with other facts about what is contextually salient) determines the semantic value of a quotation, it also remains a mystery how we are able to go from a quotation to what it quotes (we pursue this point further in Ch. 8).

We grant, of course, that the proximity requirement is vague, and so one might choose not to put much weight on it. That said, it certainly would be a strength of a theory were it to capture this intuition in an interesting way. Semantic construals of QCS seem not to be in a position to do that.

7.1.3. Over-Generation

A third consideration against some of the data in support of QCS is that it makes false predictions about what we can say using quotation expressions, as least on a liberal construal of the flexibility data, as suggested by some of García-Carpintero's data (in particular, cases (7.4)–(7.5)).

On the assumption that quotation is context sensitive, it follows that what a quotation expression quotes on any occasion is determined either by speaker intentions or by what is contextually salient. There isn't anything else on offer.

According to García-Carpintero (and others), quotation expressions quote not only types but also tokens, as in (7.4)–(7.5). We have no complaint against an audience being directed to a token with an utterance of a quotation expression. But, just the same, we find it rather difficult, more difficult than it ought to be were there unrestricted support for QCS available, to retrieve true utterances of a quotation sentence like (7.9):

7.9. 'a' ≠ 'a'.

Were García-Carpintero right, it should be no harder to render an utterance of (7.9) true than one of (7.10):

7.10. That ≠ that.

If a speaker intends to refer to a particular token with her first utterance of ''a'' and to an expression-type with her second, then her utterance of (7.9) is true. Or, if prior to her utterance of (7.9) the speaker had been drawing attention to differences between two particular tokens of the same quotation-expression, then her utterance should be true. However, as a matter of fact, intuitively, we and our informants find it most difficult to recover either reading of (7.9), even after we explicitly render both readings of the sentence salient.

Similar considerations extend to readings of other quotation sentences whose truth seems to require quoted-tokens, as in (7.11)–(7.12):

> 7.11. 'I' didn't exist twenty seconds ago.
> 7.12. 'I' tastes like peach.

The impossibility (or at least the great difficulty) we and our informants confront in retrieving true readings of utterances of (7.11)–(7.12) provides at least some evidence against the unrestricted scope of QCS. Quotational usage, as a matter of fact, simply lacks the flexibility that an unconstrained construal of QCS predicts.[7]

We turn to our final objections to a semantic explanation of the data in support of QCS.

7.1.4. Indirect Reports and Collectivity

In Cappelen and Lepore (2004), we pressed into service a number of tests in order to identify (semantic) context sensitivity in natural language. We'll discuss two (others can be found *ibid* ch. 7): namely, the Inter-Contextual Disquotational Indirect Reporting Test and the Collectivity Test.

'Inter-Contextual Disquotational Indirect Reporting' is an ugly label for the following unexceptional phenomenon. Take an utterance u of a sentence S by speaker A in context C. An inter-contextual disquotational indirect report of u is an utterance u' in a context C' (where C' ≠ C) of 'A said that S.' In Cappelen and Lepore (2004), we defended using such reports to test for context sensitivity. More explicitly, we proposed the following test:

---

[7] We should point out that these intuitions alone, even if correct, do not rule out a semantic construal for all the variability data in support of QCS. They don't rule out, for example, the possibility that distinct types can be quoted on distinct occasions of use (and so, they don't rule out, for example, García-Carpintero's cases (7.1)–(7.3) and (7.6)).

Inter-contextual Disquotational Indirect Reporting Test: If an occurrence of an expression e in a sentence S tends to block disquotational indirect reports (i.e. tends to render them false), then that's evidence that e, and so S, is (semantically) context-sensitive.

Utterances of sentences containing the first-person pronoun 'I' cannot be disquotationally indirectly reported (except by self-reporters). If Bill tries to report Frank's utterance of 'I am Italian' with 'Frank said that I am Italian', he'll fail. Utterances of sentences containing the word 'today' cannot be disquotationally reported (except by same-day reporters). If Bill tries today to report Frank's utterance yesterday of 'John will leave today' with 'Frank said that John will leave today', he'll fail. Utterances of sentences with the demonstrative expression 'that' cannot be disquotationally reported (except by co-demonstrating reporters). If Bill, while pointing at a car, tries to report on Frank's utterance of 'That's lovely'—where Frank was pointing at a table, he'll fail.

In the reverse direction, suppose you suspect expression e is context-*in*sensitive. Take an utterance u of a sentence S containing e in context C. And let C′ be a context relevantly different from C (e.g. different speakers, different times, different demonstrated objects, different speaker intentions, different salience conditions, and so on). If there's a true disquotational indirect report of u in C′, then that's evidence that S, and so e, are context-*in*sensitive.[8]

For an illustration of how this test applies to quotation expressions, consider three contexts C1–C3 varying however you like. In each, suppose that you utter (7.1).

7.1. 'gone' is dissyllabic.

We'll now engage in actual speech acts: The indented items below represent actual utterances made by us in our study. These are acts where we are reporting on your three utterances of (7.1):

In C1, you said that 'gone' is dissyllabic.
In C2, you said that 'gone' is dissyllabic.
In C3, you said that 'gone' is dissyllabic.

Our claim is that we can report your utterances of (7.1) without remembering or even ever knowing any particulars about their original contexts of utterance. In particular, we need not have extensive knowledge of:

---

[8] For further discussion of this test, see Cappelen and Lepore (2006).

- your intentions;
- your audience's intentions;
- the nature of the conversation that you and your audience were engaged in;
- the assumptions you shared with your audience;
- what was contextually salient in your original context of utterance; and
- the perceptual inputs of you and your audience in your original context of utterance.

If we're right, this provides some very strong evidence that quotation is *not* (semantically) context-sensitive; i.e. it provides some strong evidence against a semantic construal of the data in support of QCS.

We turn to our second test for semantic context sensitivity.

Collectivity Test: If a noun e is (semantically) context-sensitive (i.e. if it changes *semantic* value from one context of utterance to another), then on the basis of merely knowing there are two contexts of utterance, one in which 'e is F' is true and the other in which 'e is G' is true, we *cannot* automatically infer that there is a third context in which 'e is F and G' is true.

As an illustration, suppose there are two contexts, one in which 'You are hungry' is true and one in which 'You are thirsty' is true (and suppose further that we know little about these contexts; pertinently, we don't know the addressee of the contexts). In such circumstances, we surely couldn't infer there is a third context in which 'You are hungry and thirsty' is true. The word 'you' does not admit of blind collection. The test can be reworded so as to apply to all the other familiar sorts of context-sensitive expressions, regardless of grammatical status (see Cappelen and Lepore 2004: Ch. 7) for the details).

Returning to quotation expressions, recall García-Carpintero's examples (7.1) and (7.3).

7.1. 'Gone' is dissyllabic.
7.3. 'Gone' sounds nice.

According to him, whereas with an utterance of (7.1), the quotation expression can refer to an expression, with an utterance of (7.3) it can refer to a different type somehow related to the token. Even were we to grant him these data, here's evidence against a semantic construal of them.

Suppose, for the sake of argument, you know no more than that there is a context C1 in which (7.1) is true and another context C2 in which (7.3) is true. Is it your intuition that you can infer automatically that there is a third context in which (7.13) is true?

7.13. 'Gone' sounds nice and is dissyllabic.

To the extent that it's your intuition that you can, regardless of how ignorant, misinformed, or uninterested you are about the facts surrounding contexts C1 and C2, the more likely it is you will reject his claim that quotation expressions are semantically context-sensitive.[9]

The bottom line is this. Unprejudiced applications of the Indirect Disquotation Reporting and Collectively Tests (and others—see Cappelen and Lepore 2004: Ch. 7), provide strong evidence against the claim that quotation is semantically context-sensitive; and so, against a semantic construal of the data in support of QCS.

We don't deny that if you come to these data with a philosophical axe to grind, you might very well be able to screen off the relevant intuitions; our point is that from a naive perspective the reactions described above seem unimpeachable *and* nothing like this is possible for any of the traditionally accepted (semantically) context-sensitive expressions. To that extent, minimally, anyone who wants to endorse a semantic explanation for the variability intuitions about quotational usage owes an explanation for this asymmetry.

7.1.5. Preliminary Conclusion

Where have we gotten to? We concede that different information might be conveyed by the same quotation expressions on distinct occasions of use, but we take the arguments in sects. 7.1.1–7.1.4 to provide strong evidence that this variability should not be given a semantic

---

[9] It's easy to see how to extend this line of argument to the thesis that quotation expressions are ambiguous. If the quotation expression has one meaning in (7.1) and another in (7.3), then we should not be able to conjunction reduce with (7.13). But we can; and so this is at least partial evidence that there aren't different objects being quoted by the two occurrences of ''gone'' in (7.1) and (7.3) respectively. Note how absurd it would be to do this with genuinely ambiguous expressions. Imagine someone tokening 'bank' twice, once in reference to the side of a river and once in reference to a financial institution. He says on one occasion 'John keeps his money in the bank' and on another 'John keeps his boat on the bank.' No one would be tempted, except possibly as a joke, to conjunction reduce these *salva veritate* into 'John keeps his money in, and his boat on, the bank.'

explanation. On the assumption that these arguments are sound, we need an alternative explanation for the remaining variability data. We turn to that task directly.

7.2. PRAGMATIC EXPLANATIONS OF QCS ALONG WITH RECALCITRANT DATA

The arguments in sect. 7.1 establish that the data in support of QCS should not be explained semantically. The task of this section is to explore an alternative strategy for accommodating these data. We proceed, first, by outlining three more or less familiar pragmatic strategies for explaining data about communicated content that is not part of semantic content of the sentence uttered, suggesting how these strategies can account for some of the variability data. Then we'll argue that some of quotational variability data resist even a pragmatic explanation.

7.2.1. Pragmatic Strategies for Explaining Variability Data

Here are three familiar strategies for explaining intuitions about a sentence S varying in truth-value across contexts of utterance even though S isn't semantically context-sensitive:

- **Strategy 1: Conversational Implicature:** In some of the cases cited in support of a semantic explanation of the data behind QCS, we could say that what the speaker *said* is false, but that what she conversationally *implicated* is true. For example, we might opt to read García-Carpintero's example (7.5) (already dismissed as an illegitimate case of semantic-context sensitivity):

  7.5 At least one of these words is heavier than 'gone'

  (which you are supposed to imagine written in big wooden letters) so that its utterances semantically expresses a false content (i.e. assuming the semantic value of 'gone' is abstract, and so lacks weight). But, just the same, a speaker can expect her audience, by virtue of recognizing its obvious absurdity, to infer conversationally that a contextually salient token has a weight.

- **Strategy 2: Speech Act Pluralism:** Alternatively, if you agree with us (and others)[10] that an utterance of a sentence S (literally) asserts

---

[10] See e.g. Cappelen and Lepore 1997*a*; 2004: Ch. 13, and Soames 2002, 2005.

a plurality of propositions, only one of which is semantically expressed,[11] then you can say about the cases in question that they literally assert truths. Since these truths need not be the semantic content of S, we need not infer anything about the semantic context sensitivity of quotation. On this view, it is possible for an utterance of a sentence S containing a quotation expression Q (literally) to make an assertion about a token, even though that is not the semantic content of S and Q.

- **Strategy 3: Pragmatic Ellipsis:** In some cases, an appeal to ellipsis might explain the data. An utterance of (7.5) might be elliptical for (7.5.1):

> 7.5.1. At least one of these words is heavier than this token of 'gone'.

How attractive this option seems to you will depend on what your favorite theory of ellipsis says.[12]

Our goal in what follows is not to choose among these three or other pragmatic strategies. As we see the situation, the arguments of sect. 7.1 rule out a semantic construal of the data in support of QCS. The question that remains is which available non-semantic strategy explains the intuitions about the legitimate variability data.

Pragmatic Strategies 1–3 are familiar (enough) and can be applied in rather obvious ways to explain some of these data. The goal of the remainder of this section is to establish the need for a fourth strategy—neither semantic nor pragmatic. The reason why we bother, given that Pragmatic Strategies 1–3 are available, is because some variability data presented in support of QCS resist pragmatic interpretation (we discuss these in sect. 7.2.2 below) and these cases are, we think, the most intriguing aspects of the variability data.

7.2.2. Recalcitrant Data

A problem conveniently skirted in sect. 7.1 is that some of the variability cases canvassed in support of QCS permit *neither* easy indirect disquotational reporting *nor* collection of prior uses. We focus on such cases

---

[11] Note that on some versions of speech act pluralism, you needn't assert semantic content. See Cappelen and Lepore (2004: Ch. 13).

[12] Not in the syntactic sense, but in the sense of Sellars (1954: 198 ff.) and Neale (2000: 187).

in what follows because they clarify the shortcoming of a pragmatic construal of QCS, and they also are, quite frankly, puzzling, since they might at first glance seem to support a semantic construal of QCS—a thesis we have already provided (what we take to be) strong evidence against.

Consider a variation on García-Carpintero's (7.6):

7.6.1. 'Madrid' = '**Madrid**'.

Note that different fonts (and font sizes) are used on the right- and left-hand sides of the identity sign in (7.6.1)—Times Roman, on the left hand side, and Verdana, on the right. It easy enough to imagine contexts in which we would have the intuition that an utterance of (7.6.1) is true, and others in which, intuitively, it is not.

Imagine (7.6.1) tokened in a context C where the speaker is typing a rather obvious identity, but mid-sentence some strange formatting button is unintentionally pushed on the computer which switches the font from Times Roman to Verdana (and where the font makes no difference to the writer at all—she doesn't know what font she's writing in, doesn't know that it changed mid-sentence, and wouldn't care if she did). Intuition is that the resulting utterance of (7.6.1) is true.

Imagine, next, (7.6.1) tokened in a context C′, where the writer is intending to bring to her audience's attention the differences between the Times Roman and Verdana. She might utter (7.6.1) as a test case to her audience. In this context it's easy enough to provoke the intuition that (7.6.1) is false.

Here's the puzzle: these data seem to *pass* our tests for semantic context sensitivity. That is, they permit neither collection nor indirect disquotational reporting. Try collecting the imagined true token of (7.6.1) in C and the imagined true token of its negation (7.14) in C′ into a true token of (7.15), say, in C′′:

7.14. 'Madrid' ≠ '**Madrid**'.
7.15. 'Madrid' = '**Madrid**' and 'Madrid' ≠ '**Madrid**'.

You can't do it without seemingly falling into incoherence.

As for indirect disquotational reports, try to report a written token of (7.13) (uttered in C′) in spoken language (i.e. let the indirect report of the written utterance of (7.14) in C′ be spoken) in a context C′′. You can't do it without running into obvious difficulties. A spoken medium simply doesn't permit us (semantically) to express by mere disquotation of (7.14) what's going on in these sorts of cases. Or, suppose your keyboard lacks distinct fonts. It would seem that you couldn't even indirectly disquotationally report a token of (7.14) graphemically.

How are we to explain (away) these puzzling data? A semantic story is off the table for reasons provided in sect. 7.1. But invoking Pragmatic Strategies 1–3 is not going to be of much help in these contexts either.

Suppose we try to argue, for example, that one of (7.6.1) or (7.14) is false. If so, which one? And what could be the reason for choosing it and not its counterpart as the false one? Suppose we choose (7.6.1) as the false one on the basis of its quotable items being physically type-distinct. That could render every identity between quotational expressions false. Or, suppose we try to argue that, contrary to intuition, a spoken indirect disquotational report of (7.14) is as a matter of fact true. The extreme implausibility of this view makes such a position exceedingly unattractive. Similarly, suppose we try to argue that (7.6) or (7.6.1) is false. If this were so, should we conclude that (7.16) (with two quotation expressions in the same font but with one in normal print and the other in bold print) and infinitely many like identities are also false?

7.16. 'Madrid' = '**Madrid**'

And what about (7.17) (with two quotation expressions written in the same font but in different font sizes) and infinitely many like identities of different font sizes? Are they also all false?

7.17. 'Madrid' = 'Madrid'.

Our inability to make a reasonable non-arbitrary choice here indicates how the pragmatic strategies fail in explaining this part of the variability data. It would seem that we can't really progress any further towards an explanation of these data until we devise something that has been transparently lacking in the discussion thus far—namely, an account of how quotation expressions themselves are to be individuated. Are the two quotation expressions in (7.16) and (7.17) the same or identical? And if we can't answer these questions, then we have no satisfactory answer to the question of whether in (7.6) or (7.6.1) the quotation expressions are identical or distinct.

7.4. CONCLUSION AND PROMISSORY NOTE

In this chapter, we did not try to account for the recalcitrant data or attempt to answer the puzzling question raised by examples such as

(7.6.1) and (7.14). We'll keep our readers on the edge of their seats in breathless suspense on these issues until Ch. 12. We put this task off until the last chapter of the book because we first need to articulate our positive theory in Ch. 11 in order to present our explanation of these puzzle cases adequately.

What we take ourselves to have achieved in this chapter is establishing that a semantic construal of the variability data in support of QCS is out of the question. Any semantic theory that makes quotation semantically context-sensitive is mistaken. This will play a crucial role in what follows. It will help us refute the Use Theories of Quotation in Ch. 8 and Davidson's Demonstrative Theory of Quotation in Ch. 9. It will also mandate an important constraint on the positive theory of Ch. 11.

PART II

THEORIES

In the next four chapters, we turn from data to theory. We will discuss and evaluate five distinct theories of quotation: the Use Theory (Ch. 8), the Name and Description Theories (Ch. 9), the Demonstrative Theory (Ch. 10), and the Minimal Disquotational Theory (Ch. 11). Our criticism of the first four theories will rely heavily on the discussions in Part I. In each case we will conclude that the theory runs counter to what we have argued in Chs. 3–7 is the correct view of the basic data. So it might become clearer at this point why some of the issues in Part I mattered to us. Arguments seemingly innocent when discussed in a non-theoretical context will suddenly take on a larger significance. It's methodologically important, we think, to have evaluated these data points in as neutral an environment as possible.

These four chapters will provide a kind of overview of the theories of quotation that have been proposed over the last century. Some of these theories we could have refuted very quickly or ignored completely. But it is important, we think, to have a somewhat comprehensive overview of the different positions in logical space. Only after recognizing (as we have done the hard way) how difficult it is to accommodate all the data surveyed in earlier chapters can you see the attractiveness of the view developed in Ch. 11.

8

Use Theories

8.1. USE THEORIES: QUOTATION AS A DERIVATIVE PHENOMENON

One relatively recent and yet influential development in the literature on quotation is a class of theories that we shall call *Use Theories*, though no Use Theorist actually employs the term. The more common label is 'the Identity Theory'—first used, as far as we know, by Washington (1992), though he attributes the view to Frege (1892) and Searle (1969). However, the passages on which he bases his attributions hardly count as presenting, much less as defending, a theory of quotation; they read more like dogmatic pronouncements (more below). Since Washington (1992), Use Theories have been developed in greater detail by Saka (1998, 1999, 2005), Reimer (1996, 2005), Recanati (2001), and others.

Washington's presentation of the Identity Theory is surprisingly compressed ('succinct' would be more charitable). He says:

The quotation as a whole is analyzed into the marks that signify quotational use of the quoted expression and the quoted expression itself used to mention an object. All expressions, even those whose standard uses are not as mentioning expressions, become mentioning expressions in quotation . . . a quoted expression is related to its value by identity: a quoted expression mentions itself. (Washington 1992: 557)

There are five crucial components here:

1. We begin with the idea that the practice of quotation with quotation marks (as in (1.1)–(1.4)) is a derivative phenomenon.

    1.1. 'Snow is white' is true in English iff snow is white.

    1.2. 'Aristotle' refers to Aristotle.

    1.3. 'The' is the definite article in English.

    1.4. 'Bachelor' has eight letters.

2. The basic phenomenon is what can, in a neutral terminology, be called *quotational usage* (*or metalinguistic usage*). On this view, when words are used with certain intentions, they are being used quotationally, and on such occasions they are not being used with their usual meanings or extensions.

3. Quotation marks function merely as conventional indicators of quotational usage; they signal that the expressions within quotation marks are being used quotationally.

4. What's quoted by a quotational use of language (i.e. by the special kind of usage indicated by quotation marks) is determined by speaker intentions and various salient features of the context of utterance.

5. Quotation marks are eliminable and what results is grammatical. On this view, (4.4) and (8.1) are grammatical and true (at least when spoken):[1]

4.4. Donald is Davidson's name.

8.1. Runs is a verb.

There are, according to Use Theorists, no missing (or implicit) quotation marks in (4.4) and (8.1). Quotation marks in written language function simply to indicate words are being used in this special, quotational way, i.e. not with their regular extensions.

The conjunction of (1)–(5) serves as an idealized version of the Use Theory.

Proponents differ on how they elaborate these points, on how they defend them, and on how to weigh them.[2] We will argue that (1)–(5) should be rejected (some of our arguments have already been advanced in earlier chapters and we will simply remind you of them here).

8.2. TERMINOLOGY: 'IDENTITY THEORY' VS. 'USE THEORY'

There's a lot of discussion in the literature of what's labeled 'the Identity Theory'. The 'identity' component is picked up from the formulation, 'a

---

[1] Use Theorists differ over whether quotation marks are needed in writing; it is hard, however, for us to discern a fundamental difference.

[2] Recanati (2001), e.g., is not explicit in his endorsement of (5) except for mixed quotes. However the spirit of his view indicates he should endorse (5) for all quotations.

quoted expression is related to its value by identity: a quoted expression mentions itself' (Washington 1992: 605). This formulation, however, is deeply misleading (Washington agrees with us in pers. comm.), since according to both Washington (and other Use Theorists such as Recanati and Saka), quotational usage can refer to types, tokens, or shapes (see *ibid.* 594). So, the label is misleading in that there is no identity between what's quoted and what it quotes. It is not the case that in quotation, every expression e refers to (or quotes) e. Sometimes an expression e can be used quotationally to refer to a token or a concept or a shape or what have you.

'Identity Theory' is misleading in another respect: it is misleading to say that it is the expression itself that is doing the referring. That's true *only* when liberally construed as follows: there's no *semantic* rule for quotation marks. Quotation marks indicate that the quoted expression—when used—is being used in a special quotational way. The expression itself has no referring role; it is more informative to say it is *the speaker* who refers by virtue of using an expression in a quotational way (say, with a quotational/mentioning intention). So what a token of the expression refers to depends on the speaker intentions of whoever produces the token.

Before we engage in a critical discussion of the Use Theory, we will present in more detail what we take to be the two most serious versions of this kind of theory (to illustrate how flesh can be put on the conjunction of (1)–(5))—namely, Saka's and Recanati's Use Theories respectively—and then we'll go on to say a bit more about the alleged historical precedence of these views in Frege and Searle.

8.3. SAKA'S USE THEORY

In a series of papers, Saka develops a theory that incorporates three basic ideas: (a) there is a difference between use and mention; (b) quotation marks are just indicators of mention; and (c) quotation marks are ambiguous/indeterminate, and so can be used to refer to different things. We begin with his discussion of mentioning.

For Saka, mentioning an expression is more basic than quoting it, where the latter is defined by an appeal to the former. He defines 'mentioning' as follows:

(m) Speaker S mentions an expression X iff

I. S exhibits a token of X;

II. *S* thereby ostends the multiple items associated with *X*;

III. *S* intends to direct the thoughts of his audience to some item associated with *X* other than its extension.   (Saka 1998: 126)

So, for example, among the multiple items associated with the word 'cat' are an orthographic form, a phonetic form, a lexical entry, an intention, and an extension. When someone utters this word, according to Saka, she 'directly ostends or exhibits the phonic token . . . [and] deferringly ostends the corresponding form type, the lexeme . . . , noun, the concept CAT, the customary reference, etc.' (*ibid.*). In the case of mentioning, the speaker intends to direct her audience to some item saliently associated with 'cat' other than its (normal) extension, that is, one of the other items listed above.

Since it is a matter of speaker intentions, on this account mentioning it is not a semantic phenomenon; it 'is a purely pragmatic affair' (*ibid.* 128). It is a kind of speech act: exhibiting tokens in order to direct one's audience towards a certain kind of object (namely, the object that the speaker has in mind 'associated' with the term's extension).

An expression on this account of course, can be mentioned without employing quotation marks. All that is required is that the speaker intends to direct her audience to an item associated with the expression other than its extension. It follows that quotation marks are at best conventional indicators of mentioning. So (4.1) 'is a grammatical and true sentence' (*ibid.* 118):

4.1. Cats is a noun.

His motivations for what might seem to some as a peculiar consequence of his view are the same as indicated in Ch. 4:

- Spoken language 'does not require quote marks'. We can read (4.1) 'without saying 'quote-unquote', without quotative intonation, and without finger-quote gestures' (*ibid.*).

- 'Quote marks are often omitted in writing as well . . . it is downright normal, outside of scholarly writing, to exclude quote marks, especially in constructions like ' "The word cats is a noun'; and even in logic publications, where one might expect the greatest exactitude, it is common for quote marks to be omitted' (*ibid.*). In such cases, according to Saka, we have mentioning without quotation marks and grammaticality has not been compromised.

What then is the function of quotation marks, according to Saka? Their function is to announce that their user is not merely using the expression in between them but is also mentioning it: 'a pair of quote marks is a concept or intension, QUOT, which ambiguously or indeterminately maps its argument expression X into some linguistic item saliently associated with X other than the extension of X' (*ibid.* 127). The sense in which quotations are 'multiply ambiguous or indeterminate' (*ibid.* 123) is that they can serve the purpose of directing an audience's attention to 'some object saliently associated with the expression other than its extension' (*ibid.*). This salient object can be a wide variety of things: a token [3.14], a type [3.15], words understood as *form–content pairings* [3.16]; lexemes understood as *words abstracted from their inflectional paradigms* [3.17]; forms, that is *spellings or pronunciations* [3.18]; and *content* both immediate [3.19] and *translated* [3.20] (*ibid.*):

3.14. 'I' refers to me.
3.15. 'I' does not refer to anyone in particular; only tokens of it do.
3.16. 'Run' is used in the third-person plural but not singular.
3.17. 'Run' refers to run, runs, ran, running.
3.18. 'Run' consists of three letters.
3.19. The concept 'premise' is the same as the concept 'premiss'.
3.20. Galileo (who spoke no English) said, 'The Earth moves!'

So construed, the distinction between quotation and non-quotation is 'a formal, grammatical affair' (*ibid.* 128); whether an expression is 'a quotation or not depend[s] on its linguistic *structure*' (*ibid.* 129). Whether an expression is *mentioned* is *not* 'a formal grammatical affair'. However, the two are closely connected since quotation explicitly marks mentioning.

One implication of this view is particularly illuminating of the distinction between quoting and mentioning: on Saka's view, a quoted expression can be either mentioned or used. If a quotation, e.g. ''cat'', is used, the speaker intends to direct the audience's attention to its extension. If it is mentioned, the speaker intends to direct the speaker's intention to an item saliently associated with ''cat'' other than its regular extension (see *ibid.* 128).

8.4. RECANATI'S USE THEORY

Recanati (2000, 2001) develops a version of the Use Theory of Quotation based on the work of Clark and Gerrig (1990). According to this view, quotation marks 'conventionally indicate the fact that the speaker is demonstrating the enclosed words' (Recanati 2001: 680). Linguistic demonstrations are central to understanding how language is used to talk about language, but Recanati is not using 'demonstration' in the sense of 'to *demonstrate* an object, using a demonstrative pronoun'. Rather, he uses it in the sense of 'to illustrate' or 'to exemplify', the sense in which you can demonstrate (illustrate, exemplify) how someone walks, dances, or utters a sentence (Recanati 2001: 640). On his view, quotation belongs with phenomena such as exaggerated tones of voice and mimicry. Recanati takes his view from Clark, and he compares Clark's and Davidson's use of 'demonstrate' in this passage:

> In contrast to Davidson, Clark uses 'demonstrate' 'in its everyday sense of 'illustrate by exemplification'' (Clark and Gerrig 1990, p. 764 fn.). In that sense, Clark says, 'you can demonstrate a tennis serve, a friend's limp, or the movement of a pendulum' (Clark and Gerrig 1990, p. 764). To do so you must yourself produce an instance of the serve, the limp, or the movement. In quotation, what we demonstrate is a piece of verbal behaviour—a way of speaking. We demonstrate it by producing an instance of that behaviour, that is, by speaking in the relevant way. (Recanati 2001: 661)

Recanati says: 'This makes quotation, at bottom, a *paralinguistic* phenomenon, like gesturing or intonation' (*ibid.*). The function of quotation marks is, as in all Use Theories, to indicate this special usage.

What is demonstrated by an utterance of a sentence containing a quotation can vary from one context of utterance to another—in this respect Recanati endorses the view that quotations are context-sensitive. For him, the demonstration involved in using a quotation typically depicts an utterance, what he calls the target utterance (ibid. 642). Of course, which utterance is targeted and which aspect of it is exemplified (or mimicked) depends on speaker intentions—in Recanati's terminology, 'the point' of the demonstration (i.e. exemplification) can vary (*ibid.* 667) and what is depicted can vary as well. In this respect, Recanati's version of the Use Theory introduces the most context sensitivity to quotation—there are at least three parameters that can shift from context to context: the target, the relevant features of the target, and the point of demonstrating those features of that target.

Recanati agrees with both Washington and Saka that this special kind of usage, what he calls demonstrative usage, where the speaker draws the audience's attention to language itself, can occur in the absence of quotation marks (see *ibid.* 662). We can, for example, demonstrate (i.e. illustrate) 'all manner of speech characteristics—speed, gender, age, dialect, accent, drunkenness, lisping, anger, surprise, fear, stupidity, and power' (Recanati 2000: 175; there he quotes Clark 1996: 175).

What all these linguistic demonstrations share is what Recanati calls 'iconicity'. Exactly what iconicity is or involves is a complicated matter (see Recanati 2001: 644–5), but the general idea is simple: linguistic demonstrations are intended to resemble, in some respect, either an actual utterance (in which case it is a form of echoing or mimicry) or an abstract type of utterance. What Recanati says about 'open quotation' makes this somewhat clearer.

Open quotes are those that are not noun phrases (he calls those 'closed quotes', see below). According to Recanati, the central fault in traditional theories of quotation is that open quotation has been ignored. Examples (8.2) and (8.3) are paradigms of open quotation:

8.2. 'Comment allez vous?' That is how you would translate 'How do you do' in French.
8.3. Stop that John! 'Nobody likes me', 'I am miserable' . . . Don't you think you exaggerate a bit?

In (8.3), tokens of 'Nobody likes me' and 'I am miserable' are displayed for demonstrative purposes (to depict a target utterance, i.e. one of John's utterances). In (8.2), a French utterance is presented for demonstrative purposes (the target being a French sentence), and then later is referred to by the demonstrative 'that'. On this view, the quotation does not refer to anything. Its purpose is to illustrate. In general, the function of open quotation is not to refer. However, there is, according to Recanati, a subset of quotation that constitutes a counter-example to this general rule. He says:

This does not mean that quotation marks have no linguistic or semantic function: What the 'quotation marks' conventionally indicate in writing is the fact that the enclosed material is displayed for demonstrative purposes rather than used in the normal way. (*Ibid.* 649).

. . . the quotation marks themselves have a linguistic meaning—they conventionally indicate the fact that the speaker is demonstrating the enclosed words. (*Ibid.* 680)

In terminology we introduced above, quotation marks are conventional indicators of metalinguistic usage.

In some cases, quotations refer. Sentences (1.4) and (8.4) exemplify what Recanati calls 'closed quotation':

1.4. 'Bachelor' has eight letters.
8.4. . . . And then Greta Garbo said, 'I want to be alone!'

In these cases, the quotation is 'linguistically recruited and assumes the role of a singular term within a sentence' (*ibid.* 650). In these cases, the quotations are singular terms that refer to a target sentence. More precisely, what refers is 'the demonstration qua-syntactically recruited' (*ibid.* 651).

A central task in Recanati exegesis is to figure out exactly what he means by the claim that a demonstration (i.e. a quotation) is recruited as a singular term (For further discussion of this point, see Recanati (2001) and Benbaji (2004*a*, 2004*b*, 2005)).

Recanati (2001: 649–50) summarizes his view thus:

> To sum up: Following Clark, I hold that quotations are linguistic demonstrations. What the 'quotation marks' conventionally indicate in writing is the fact that the enclosed material is displayed for demonstrative purposes rather than used in the normal way. But neither the displayed material nor the target of the demonstration (whether distal or proximal) is referred to, unless the quotation happens to be 'closed', that is, unless it acquires the grammatical function of a singular term within a sentence in which it fills a slot. When that is the case, the quotation transformed into a singular term acquires a referential value. Because the demonstration acquires a referential value in such cases, most theorists have jumped to the conclusion that quotations in general refer to what they depict. But that is not true. Only closed quotations refer. Open quotations merely depict.

One final remark about Recanati's view: the target of a quotation, i.e. that which it (i.e. the demonstration) attempts to mimic or echo (or, more generally, be an icon of), can vary from context to context. It depends, for example, on what the target utterance is (this will be determined in context) and what features of that target utterance are being mimicked. In general, this is a theory that leaves even more to be determined by speaker intentions than Saka's view. In (1.10), for example,

1.10. Quine said that quotation 'has a certain anomalous feature'.

Recanati (*ibid.* 667) says:

> the ascription of the quoted words to the person whose speech or thought is reported is not even a conventional implicature. It belongs to the most

pragmatic layer of interpretation, where one tries to *make sense of the speaker's act of demonstration in the broader context in which it takes place*. This is not 'interpretation' in the narrowly linguistic sense. (our emphasis)

8.5. THE HISTORY OF USE THEORIES: FREGE, SEARLE, AND THE PICTURE THEORY

Washington, Recanati, and Saka are our paradigms of Use Theorists, but before proceeding to a critical discussion of their theories, some history is appropriate. Use Theorists tend to trace their view back to Frege. The passage quoted in support of this distinguished pedigree is the following:

If words are used in the ordinary way, what one intends to speak of is what they mean. It can also happen however, that one wishes to talk about the words themselves or their sense. This happens, for instance, when the words of another are quoted. One's own words then first designate words of the other speaker, and only the latter have their usual meaning. We then have signs of signs. In writing, the words are in this case enclosed in quotation marks. Accordingly, a word standing between quotation marks must not be taken as having its ordinary meaning. (Frege 1892: 201)

It is not at all clear to us that this passage supports a Use Theory. For one thing, there's no mention of a special quotational use. We take that to be essential. Frege also says something puzzling about what the quoted words designate: he says they 'designate words of the other speaker'. That makes it seem as if they do not designate the words (or word types) themselves. How to interpret that phrase is tricky, not something we will pursue further.

What is clear is that there's no way to understand the passage accurately without trying to place it within the larger framework of Frege's semantics, and we have not seen that done by any Use Theorist. The only attempt to do so is Parsons (1982), and on his interpretation, Frege is clearly *not* a Use Theorist in the sense of defending (1)–(5) above.

A better case can be made that Searle is an early proponent of Use Theories. Searle (1968: 76) says that in quotation, 'a word is uttered . . . but not in its normal use. The word itself is presented and then talked about, and that it is to be taken as presented rather than used conventionally to refer is indicated by the quotes.' This certainly introduces a special quotational usage and endorses the view that quotation marks function to indicate this usage. What the passage does not incorporate is the claim that quotes are context-sensitive and grammaticality is preserved when quotation marks are eliminated—though it is hard to make sense of which syntactic function quotation marks have for Searle, given that they have no function other than to 'indicate' that the words are used a certain special way.[3]

One final historical remark: Quine said a good number of things about quotation; in one passage (1940: 26) he writes, 'a quotation is not a description but a hieroglyph; it designates its object not by describing it in terms of other objects, but by picturing it.' Davidson (1979), taking his cue from this passage and others, baptized the view suggested in Quine's passage the Picture Theory of Quotation (cf. also Christensen 1967: 362). As Davidson (1979: 83–4) notes, on this view, 'it is not the entire quotation, that is, expression named plus quotation marks that refers to the expression, but rather the expression itself. The role of the quotation marks is to indicate how we are to take the expression within: the quotation marks constitute a linguistic environment within which expressions do something special'. What Davidson is saying here, about this account at least, is that the quotation marks *per se* have no semantic function; rather, they indicate that the words are used in a special way. They are used ' 'autonomously', that is, to name itself'. So understood, the Picture Theory is exactly like the Identity Theory, and so for the same reason is a Use Theory. A Picture Theory is a Use Theory because it says that quotation marks are *in*essential; they only indicate a special use. They indicate that expressions are being used in a certain way: as a picture or as a hieroglyph. As far as we can tell, however, the Picture Theory is just another variant on a Use Theory. We will not pursue it further except inasmuch as we assume that what we have to say critical of Use Theories in general extends to the Picture Theory as well.

8.6. EVALUATION OF USE THEORIES

Our practice of using quotation can seem exceedingly flexible. We can, apparently, do some rather wild things with quotation. It appears hard, if not impossible, to find a theory that both captures the richness and apparent flexibility of this practice and isn't deeply context-dependent. In particular, it might seem tempting to ground a theory in some aspect

---

[3] Gomez-Torrente (2001) challenges the interpretation of Searle given by Washington (1992).

of speakers' intentions, just as Use Theories do. This is particularly tempting if you are convinced that quotation is a parasitic phenomenon and that quotational use (or mentioning) is at the foundation of our ability to turn language on itself. If this usage is a matter of speakers' intentions, then something like the Use Theory must be correct.

In these respects, Use Theories fall into a more general trend towards contextualism in philosophy of language and other philosophical subdisciplines. We are opposed to this slide into contextualism both in general and in the case of quotation specifically. We presented our more general objections to contextualism in Cappelen and Lepore (2004). This passage from Szabo (2006: 31) provides an excellent summary of our view:

> appeals to context sensitivity have become 'cheap'—the twenty-first century version of ordinary language philosophy's rampant postulations of ambiguity. Not only is this 'the lazy man's approach to philosophy', it undermines systematic theorizing about language. The more we believe context can influence semantic content, the more we will find ourselves at a loss when it comes to explaining how ordinary communication (let alone the transmission of knowledge through written texts) is possible.

In the case of quotation, we have provided two of our main reasons for denying Use Theories in earlier chapters. In Ch. 4, we argued against making it a condition on an adequate theory of quotation that it explain 'Quotation Without Quotation Marks'. In Ch. 7, we argued that quotation is context *in*sensitive. Those two chapters alone suffice to undermine both the motivation for Use Theories and the specific claims made in different versions of the theory. Our first two objections simply serve as reminders of what we argued in those earlier chapters. In addition, we argue that Use Theories can't account for what Saka calls 'forward and backward productivity', and lastly that these theories have undesirable syntactic implications.

Objection 1: There's No Special Quotational Usage and Even If There Were, It Would Be Irrelevant to a Semantic Theory for Quotation

We have already provided reasons for Objection 1:

(a) The data about quotational usage are irrelevant to a semantic theory for quotation; and

(b) The data are flawed or misinterpreted by those who invoke it.

As far as we can tell, if the conclusions we reached in Ch. 4 are sound, then the fundamental motivation for Use Theories is undermined: there's no evidence of a 'special quotational use of language' and even if there were, it would be irrelevant to a semantics for quotation (i.e. to genuine quotation).

Objection 2: Quotations Are Context-Insensitive

According to the versions of the Use Theory defended by Saka, Washington, Reimer, and Recanati, a quotation can shift its semantic value from one context of utterance to another, contingent on what the speaker intends to quote and what the contextually salient quotable is (in the relevant context of utterance).

In Ch. 7, we argued extensively for the conclusion, however, that quotation expressions are context-*in*sensitive. The arguments there suffice to establish that Use Theories fail. Here is a reminder of our main critical points there:

- Context-sensitive theories over-generate.
- Context-sensitive theories can't account for accurate indirect disquotational reports involving quotation expressions.
- Context-sensitive theories can't explain accurate conjunction reductions involving quotation expressions.
- Context-sensitive theories can't guarantee the truth of the strong disquotational schema for quotation.
- Context-sensitive theories can't explain the proximity relation between a quotation expression and its semantic value.

We did not entirely complete the arguments against context sensitivity in Ch. 7—there is a promissory note issued at the end of that chapter. In particular, we promised to provide an alternative account of the flexibility data that appear to support neither semantic nor pragmatic context sensitivity—we do that in Ch. 12.

Objection 3: Use Theories Can't Account for Forward and Backward Productivity

In Ch. 3, we mentioned one version of the proximity constraint due to Saka. Here is the relevant passage: 'Just as we can productively go from knowing any expression to knowing its quotation, we can go from knowing the quotation of any expression to knowing the expression itself.' (Saka 1998: 115). Saka hereby imposes two conditions on a theory of quotation:

> **Forward Productivity**: We can productively go from knowing an expression to knowing its quotation.

Reverse Productivity: We can go from knowing the quotation of an expression to knowing the expression itself.

Saka criticizes a number of theories for not satisfying this condition and claims his theory can satisfy it. How does Saka's Use Theory satisfy the Reverse Productivity condition? Here is what he says (*ibid.* 132): 'If you are party to the convention [i.e. conventions (1)–(5) spelled out above], then knowing any expression will enable you to know its quotation; and knowing any quotation will enable you to know what is quoted.' Notice that the claim that knowing a quotation will enable you *to know what is being quoted* is at the core of Saka's claim to have satisfied the Reverse Productivity condition. That claim, however, is inconsistent with another central part of Saka's Use Theory: his claim that quotation is context-sensitive. At the end of his paper he summarizes his view as what he calls 'Multiplicity' (*ibid.*):

> MULTIPLICITY: With quotation you can refer to both linguistic expressions and non-linguistic vocalizations and imprints; to both form and content; to both types and tokens.

Given Saka's incorporation of productivity it follows that:

- Knowing a quotation expression does *not* automatically enable you to know what is quoted. You can encounter an utterance of a sentence containing a quotation of 'gone', but still have no idea what it refers to; you can see it on a page, hear it in a conversation, and still be at a complete loss as to what it quotes. It could, after all, quote anything from an expression to a token to a concept. The quotation expression itself gives very little away.

- To see how counter-intuitive Saka's view is, note that there's nothing in his view that prevents ' 'Jason' ' from quoting 'Quine'. Remember, according to Saka (*ibid.* 127), a quotation '. . . maps its argument expression X into some linguistic item saliently associated with X other than the extension of X.' There are certainly contexts in which 'Quine' is saliently associated with 'Jason'. In such contexts, ' 'Jason' ' would (or at least could) quote 'Quine'. But that's absurd. ' 'Jason' ' can never quote 'Quine'; only ' 'Quine' ' can quote 'Quine'.

This point generalizes: any Use Theorist who insists upon quotation being context sensitive will be unable to account for what Saka calls 'Reverse Productivity'. (This is particularly bad for Saka since he makes such a great deal out of this principle in his criticisms of others.)

Of course, a Use Theorist could claim 'knowing the quotation' means something more then encountering it in an utterance. But what else could it mean? Saka doesn't tell us, but one thing it could not mean is 'knowing what it refers to' since that would render a solution for the Reverse Productivity problem for any theory of quotation. On any theory, if you know what a quotation expression refers to, then you know what it refers to! So 'knowing a quotation' can't mean that. It is hard to see how to spell out the notion of 'knowing a quotation' in a non-question-begging way so that it can respect Backwards Productivity. We will try to do so in Ch. 11.

Objection 4: Use Theories Have Problematic Syntactic Implications

Remember, according to Saka (*ibid.* 118), (8.1) 'is a grammatical and true sentence.'

8.1. Runs is a noun.

Saka differs from e.g. Washington in that he holds that even a written token of (8.1) is true and grammatical; for Washington, only its spoken utterances can be true and grammatical. As far as we can tell, Saka holds the more consistent view here, given the background theory and the kind of data Use Theorists invoke. But putting that disagreement aside, we can ask: What is the syntactic category of 'runs' in (8.1)? We know 'runs' is a verb. We don't pretend to be linguistic authorities, but surely verbs can't be subjects. So, if (8.1) is grammatical, then 'runs' can't be a verb. Two strategic options are available to the Use Theorist:

1. He could say that 'runs' is not just a verb; it is also a noun—and by implication, every expression is a noun including 'or', 'the', 'every', and 'fast'. (Washington suggested something like this to us in conversation.)
2. Or, he could give up on the idea that (8.1) is grammatical.

The first option is particularly unattractive, and each requires substantial changes in how we think about English syntax. Use Theorists owe us an elaboration of how they think these changes should be realized without making a mockery of contemporary linguistic theory.

8.7. CONCLUSION

Use Theories have a kind of initial attractiveness. There are a great variety of uses to which speakers put quotations and the pragmatic flexibility that these theories leave room for seems to fit that variety well. However, if we are right, this is but another instance of a philosopher's giving in to the temptation to 'go contextualist' in order to account for linguistic data. More careful investigation of the data shows that there's a level of content that's stable and that much of what appears to be evidence in favor of the contextualist position evaporates on closer inspection.

We end this chapter by emphasizing a general methodological point. It should be clear by now that our practice of quotation incorporates a wide array of exceedingly confusing and complex data. We doubt that any theory will be able to account for all of this in anything remotely like an elegant and simple manner. No doubt, any theory will have to bite the bullet at certain points. Applied to our criticism of Use Theories, this means we don't take the above considerations to constitute knockdown objections. We've based our arguments on controversial interpretations of the data (in Chs. 4–6), and on arguments that presuppose broad agreement about the nature of semantic content (e.g. the tests appealed to in establishing semantic insensitivity in Ch. 7). There's room for disputing all of this. The primary goal of this book is to present the data (or puzzles, depending on how you see it), the costs of various theories, and a theory that we think, overall, is the most elegant and explanatory. As we see it, the problems facing Use Theories are just too overwhelming for the theory to be worth salvaging.

9

The Proper Name and the Definite Description Theories

9.1. NAMES, DESCRIPTIONS, AND SEMANTIC STRUCTURE

According to Neale (1993: 90),

> (NC) Every meaningful noun phrase (NP) in natural language is either a semantically unstructured, referring expression (singular term) or else a semantically structured, restricted quantifier.

Neale is not the only philosopher attracted to (NC) and views like it. It is an implicit assumption in a great deal of work done in philosophy of language since Frege and Russell. Discussions on quotation show how ingrained (NC) is in the semantics literature: over and over again we find semanticists trying to squeeze quotation into one of these two categories. We discuss these theories in this and the next chapter.

According to Quine and Tarski, quotations lack semantic structure. (Their position is often misleadingly called 'the Proper Name Theory'.) According to (other passages by) Quine and Tarski, and also Geach, quotations are structured definite descriptions. The Definite Description Theory fails for reasons very similar to those that undermine the Proper Name Theory, and so both theories are discussed in this chapter. Davidson's Demonstrative Theory of Quotation is also a version of the definite description theory of quotation; and though it fails for some of the same reasons the other two theories fail, because it has been so influential and because its shortcomings are so interestingly different, we will devote an entire separate chapter to discussing and evaluating it—Ch. 10.

9.2. PROPER NAME THEORY: NO SEMANTIC STRUCTURE

In the literature on quotation, there are frequent references to (and refutations of) a view often labeled 'the Proper Name Theory' (see e.g. Davidson 1979, Cappelen and Lepore 1997*b*, Reimer 1996, Washington 1992, Recanati 2001, Saka 1998). The label is *not* particularly helpful given that plethora of competing theories about the semantics for proper names. To say that quotations are proper names just isn't very informative from a semantic perspective. However, what is crucial about the Proper Name Theory is that its proponents treat quotations as *unstructured singular terms*.

The view that quotation expressions are unstructured singular terms is typically attributed to Quine[1] and to Tarski on the basis of passages like those below (see e.g. Quine 1940: 23–6; 1961*b*: 140; Tarski 1933: 159 ff.; for other historical references see also Reichenbach 1947: 335 and Carnap 1947: 4). Quine (1940: 26) writes:

From the standpoint of logical analysis each whole quotation must be regarded as a single word or sign, whose parts count for no more than serifs or syllables.

The personal name buried within the first word of the statement . . .

'Cicero' has six letters,

e.g. is logically no more germane to the statement than is the verb 'let' which is buried within the last word.

Tarski (1933: 159) writes:

Quotation-mark names may be treated like single words of a language, and thus like syntactically simple expressions. The single constituents of these names—the quotation marks and the expressions standing between them—fulfill the same function as the letters and complexes of successive letters in single words. Hence they can possess no independent meaning. Every quotation-mark name is then a constant individual name of a definite expression (the expression enclosed by the quotation marks) and is in fact a name of the same nature as the proper name of a man.

The central feature of this view is that quotations are unstructured expressions and that, as a result, the expression quoted is *not* a component of a quotation expression itself. This is obviously not an intuitive view

---

[1] Bennett (1988) reports that Quine maintained, in personal communication, that in his writings he used the term 'name' for expressions that are semantically simple.

to defend, but it did achieve the results that both Quine and Tarski desired of a theory of quotation: it explains (D1), i.e. it explains why co-referential, and even synonymous, expressions cannot be substituted for one another inside a quotation expression *salva veritate*, since, according to the Proper Name Theory, the name 'Cicero' does *not* occur in the quotation expression ''Cicero''. So, on the basis of the identity that Cicero = Tully, the name 'Tully' cannot be substituted for the name 'Cicero' in ''Cicero''. As Quine (1961*b*: 141) so aptly puts it, '[t]o make substitution upon a personal name, within such a context, would be no more justifiable than to make a substitution upon the term 'cat' within the context 'cattle''. The theory also accounts for (D2), i.e. it prohibits quantifying in, since each quotation is a simple unstructured name and so there is nothing to quantify into. To see why this is so, think of the left and right quotation marks as the 27th and 28th letters of the Roman alphabet, and then quantifying into (1.4) in deriving (3.1) makes about as much sense as trying to derive (9.3) from (9.1) and (9.2) by quantifying into both of them:

1.4. 'bachelor' has eight letters.

3.1. $(\exists x)('x'$ has eight letters)

9.1. There is a birth dearth in Europe.

9.2. Earth is the third planet from the sun.

9.3. $(\exists x)(x$ is the third planet from the sun & there is a birth dx in Europe)

The occurrence of the 24th letter of the alphabet in (3.1), as Quine notes for a similar sentence, 'is as irrelevant to the quantifier that precedes it as is the occurrence of the same letter in the context 'six'' (*ibid.*).

The Proper Name Theory also seems to account quite nicely for adequacy condition (D3) by virtue of permitting the creation of novel quotation expressions much as natural languages permit the unbounded and free introduction of novel proper names.

9.3. WEAKNESSES OF THE VIEW OF QUOTATIONS AS UNSTRUCTURED SINGULAR TERMS

It is a tradition in the literature on quotation to include a brief dismissive discussion of the Proper Name Theory. Its problems are thought to be so severe that many authors wonder whether Quine and Tarski should even be taken to have ever endorsed the view (see e.g. Bennett 1988, Richard 1986, Saka 1998, and Gomez-Torrente 2001). Today the view gets discussed largely because of its distinguished pedigree and primarily for heuristic purposes. A common view is that examining the reasons why it is 'an utter failure' (Saka 1998: 114) reveals something deep and important about how to devise an acceptable theory of quotation.

Bennett tries to alleviate Quine's (and Tarski's) culpability for the Proper Name Theory by suggesting Quine and Tarski were 'less concerned with the details of how quotation does work than with heading off some misunderstandings about it' (Bennett 1988: 401). They were essentially in the business of emphasizing that quotations are opaque and that it is not possible to quantify into a quotation. To do this, Bennett suggests, they didn't need to develop a fully adequate positive theory.

We will leave the exegesis aside (though we find it difficult to see that Quine and Tarski could have been guilty of anything less than indifferent sloppiness) and proceed to point out central difficulties with the view that quotations are unstructured. There are (at least) four: (The main objections are due Davidson 1979: 81–3, though some were anticipated by Geach 1957: 79 ff.)

Objection 1: The Argument from Disquotation

As we have emphasized several times in this book, one feature of quotation that seems indisputable is its disquotational nature, i.e. (D5), as exemplified in (7.7):

7.7. ' 'Quine' ' quotes 'Quine'.

A theory of quotation, we said in Chs. 3 and 7, should guarantee that sentences like (7.7) are true. Quine's and Tarski's theories, however, don't ensure this. Remember, on the Proper Name Theory, 'Quine' doesn't occur as a constituent of ' 'Quine' '. If the relationship between a quotation and what it quotes were anything like the relationship between a proper name and what it names, it should be possible to use a different quotation to quote 'Quine'. But it isn't. We can't, for instance, use the expression ' 'Jason' ' to quote 'Quine'. So, the analogy that Quine and Tarski draw between quotation expressions and proper names breaks down, and they offer no alternative suggestion for how to patch up the theory.

Objection 2: The Proximity Constraint

The Strong Disquotational Schema (SDS), as manifested in (7.7), is closely related to another characteristic feature of quotation we emphasized in Chs. 3 and 7 under (D5) as well: namely, the proximity constraint on a quotation and what it quotes. This constraint provides the basis for another objection (closely related to the last) of the Proper Name Theory.

The relationship between a proper name and what it names is arbitrary. Lobsters, for example, have different names in different languages. In Norwegian and French, they are called 'Hummer', in English 'Lobster'. It makes no sense to say one label is more correct than another. We can call lobsters whatever we want. Now consider the quotation, ' 'Lobster' '. It is not arbitrary that this quotation quotes what it quotes.

In Ch. 3, we canvassed three distinct ways in which philosophers have tried to spell out this special relationship: namely, Containment, Picturing, and Backwards–Forwards productivity. In some sense, the expression 'lobster' is 'in' ' 'lobster' '. In some sense, ' 'lobster' ' pictures (or is an icon or a hieroglyph of) 'lobster'. In some sense, we can go from knowing 'lobster' to knowing what its quotation is, and vice versa.

In a rather obvious sense, the Quine–Tarski Proper Name Theory can't account for these features of quotation. By virtue of saying that 'lobster' doesn't occur in ' 'lobster' ', their theory sacrifices any resources for explaining this special relationship in any of these ways.

Objection 3: The Argument from Infinitude

It is true that if quotation expressions were like proper names, we could introduce them at will. But it is also true that if they were proper names, then they would lack any semantic structure whatsoever, and so there would be no rule for determining how to generate or how to interpret a quotation expression upon encountering it for the very first time. When we stumble upon a brand new proper name, say, the name 'Alice', it's always appropriate to ask—'What (or who) does 'Alice' name?' But it makes little sense, if any at all, and it would expose a serious deficit in the comprehension of the mechanism of quotation were we to ask of the quotation expression ' 'Alice' ' what it quotes? To understand any given quotation on the Proper Name Theory would be much like learning the referent/meaning of a brand new proper name. However, the quotation ' 'acloueroeu' ', for example, can be understood by someone who has never before encountered it. Understanding it is not anything like understanding a previously unknown proper name. Upon first encountering it, you know exactly what's being referenced in a way that you do not with a proper name that you've never before encountered. In this regard, the Proper Name Theory fails to explain adequacy condition (D4). As Davidson (1979: 83) puts it, '. . . on [the Proper Name Theory] quotation mark names have no significant structure. It follows that a theory of truth could not be made to cover generally sentences containing quotations.'

Objection 4: The Proper Name Theory and Mixed Quotation

There is an objection that we ourselves pressed against the Proper Name Theory (Cappelen and Lepore 1997*b*). We were not alone in registering this complaint. Searle (1969) made the same criticism years before. What we and Searle noted in our discussions is that quotation expressions often occur in syntactic positions that do not permit the substitutions of proper names (on the assumption that proper names are noun phrases), and so quotations cannot be proper names. Here is Searle's example (1983: 185): 'note the difference between "Gerald says: 'I will consider running for the Presidency' " and "Gerald said he would 'consider running for the Presidency' ".' Inserting a name after 'would' in the second sentence results in ungrammaticality. The same objection surfaces elsewhere (cf. e.g. Simchen 1999: 326; Wertheimer 1999: 517; and Saka 1998: 120, 127).

In sum, these four objections unmask serious problems with the Proper Name Theory of Quotation. On the basis of these (and others we won't canvass here; cf. Washington 1992, Cappelen and Lepore 1997*b*, Bennett 1988), we'll quietly pass over the Proper Name Theory on to the Definite Description Theory of Quotation. We'll see that most of the same objections we raised against the Proper Name Theory extend to the Definite Description Theory as well.

9.4. QUINE AND GEACH: SEMANTIC STRUCTURE—DEFINITE DESCRIPTIONS

The defining feature of the Proper Name Theory is also its central weakness: namely, the idea that quotations are unstructured is not only intuitively implausible but it also leads to all the problems that we discussed above. That view is exclusively of historical interest—we will not pursue it further in this book. But if quotations are *not un*structured, then you can't be excused for thinking that they lack semantic structure. For those who are sympathetic with Neale's conjecture (NC), then, they must be quantifiers (since it is invariably presumed that all noun phrases are either quantifiers or unstructured referring expressions[2]). This view is exactly the view that we find in Geach and in other passages in Quine and Tarski: quotations are what Tarski called 'descriptive names'.

On the Definite Description Theory of Quotation, quotations are assimilated to definite descriptions. Since we will assume throughout this book that descriptions are quantifiers, this is a view according to which quotations are quantifiers.

There are two versions of the Definite Description Theory on the market:

a. The first is in Geach, Quine, and Tarski, for whom the semantics of a complex quotation is the same as the semantics of a definite description of a concatenation of the basic units of the quotation, where these basic units, in turn, are treated as singular unstructured referring terms.

b. The second version is in Davidson (1979) and it radically differs from the first. According to Davidson, the semantics of a quotation is assimilated to that of a definite description containing a demonstrative element, where the demonstrative refers to a token (the token that sits in between a token of the quotation marks).

View (a) fails, we will argue in this chapter, for reasons that are already present in connection with the Quine–Tarski Proper Name Theory outlined above. As a result, this version of the Definite Description Theory will be presented and discussed in the reminder of this chapter. Davidson's version, as we will see, fails for some of these same reasons, but it also fails for a more subtle reason that we will discuss in Ch. 10. Therefore, we will reserve discussion of Davidson's view until the next chapter.

9.5. THE TARSKI–QUINE–GEACH VERSION OF THE DEFINITE DESCRIPTION THEORY

The Definite Description Theory of Quotation was introduced in order to guarantee that 'a quoted series of expressions is always a series of quoted expressions' (Geach 1957: 82) and not 'a single long word,

---

[2] We will question this presumption in Ch. 11.

whose parts have no separate significance' (*ibid.*). According to this theory, there is a set of basic units in each language: words, according to Geach (*ibid.* ch. 18; 1970); letters, according to Tarski (1956: 160) and Quine (1960: 143–4, 189–90, 212).[3]

According to the Tarski–Quine version, the Proper Name Theory is correct for quotation marks appearing around letters, e.g. 'a', 'b', 'c', etc., are to be treated as primitive expressions in the language referring to the first, second, and third letters of the alphabet, and so on. Quoted expressions that are concatenations of letters (and spaces and other primitive symbols in the language) are to be treated as descriptions in the following manner. For Quine and Tarski, (1.4) gets analyzed as (9.4),

1.4. 'Bachelor' has eight letters.

9.4. 'B'-'a'-'c'-'h'-'e'-'l'-'o'-'r' has eight letters.

where the symbol '-' is their sign for concatenation, and the individual quotations are names of letters. So understood, this view retains the Proper Name Theory for basic quotation expressions, e.g. according to Quine, ''a'' is a name of one letter, ''b'' a name of another, etc.

For Geach, however, each single word has a quotation name. Complex quotations, i.e. quotations with more than one basic unit, are understood as descriptions of concatenations of the basic units. Here is an illustration from Geach (1957: 82–3) (where '&' is his sign for concatenation): . . . 'the quotation ''man is mortal'' is rightly understood only if we read it as meaning the same as '' 'man' & 'is' & 'mortal' '', i.e. read it as *describing* the quoted expression in terms of the expressions it contains and their order.' Davidson (1979: 84) characterizes the difference between the two versions: 'In primitive notation, which reveals all structure to the eye, Geach has an easier time writing (for only each word needs quotation marks) but a harder time learning or describing the language (he has a much larger primitive vocabulary—twice normal size if we disregard iteration).'

9.6. WEAKNESSES OF THE DESCRIPTION THEORY

In one respect, the Definite Description Theory is an immense improvement over the Proper Name Theory: it treats as primitives only names

---

[3] For Quine and Tarski, the Definite Description Theory was presented as an alternative to natural language quotation, and not as an analysis of natural language; this was not so for Geach, however.

of the primitive symbols of the language, which (one might reasonably assume) are finite in number, thus potentially accommodating (D3). Otherwise, however, the theory is, by a wide consensus, not much of an improvement over the Proper Name Theory. At the basic level, the theory still treats quotations as names. So, at that level, it inherits all the problems confronting the simpler Proper Name Theory and for that reason is not much more attractive. Some of the obvious objections are these (again we mention only some obvious ones here since the theory is not central to contemporary discussions):

Objection 1: The Argument from Disquotation

The first objection to the Proper Name Theory applies to what the Description Theorist thinks of as the Basic Level: at the Basic Level, the disquotational schema is not guaranteed. On Geach's view, for example, it is no more than an accident that ''Quine'' quotes 'Quine'—it could just as well have been quoted by ''Jason''. There's nothing built into the theory that guarantees this result, hence violating the strong disquotational principle SDS (from Ch. 3).

Objection 2: The Argument from Proximity

At the Basic Level, it doesn't explain the special relationship between the expression and the quotation of that expression, i.e. it fails to account for (D5). It's obvious to us that ''Sam'' and ''Alice'' do not refer to the same expression, but how can Geach explain this triviality if both are just proper names? The same applies to Quine for ''a'' and ''b'' (cf. Davidson 1979: 87; see also Objection 2 to the Proper Name Theory).

Objection 3: The Argument from Infinitude

At the Basic Level (i.e. the level of words or letters), there's no rule for determining how to interpret and generate novel quotations (D4). (See Objection 3 to the Proper Name Theory.)

Objection 4: The Argument from Mixed Quotation

Davidson also objects to the theory because it cannot provide an account of cases of mixed quotation. For if it treats expressions like ''Aristotle'' (that is, the quote name of 'Aristotle') as abbreviations for descriptions of the configuration of letters, then, semantically, there is no word which could be both used and mentioned in any sentence in which it appears. (Note that, implicitly, this assumes we need a uniform account of pure and mixed uses of quotation marks, i.e. that no semantic ambiguity is involved.) (See Objection 4 to the Proper Name Theory.)

9.7. CONCLUSION

So it looks like Neale's (NC) is in trouble. Quotation appears to provide a quite obvious counter-example to it. Quotation expressions don't fit easily into either of the two categories Neale claims that all noun phrases belong to (and quotation expressions are, at least sometimes, noun phrases). The versions of the Proper Name and Description Theories discussed in this chapter were at the centre of the semantics for quotation until Davidson's paper 'Quotation'. Since then there have been few, if any, attempts to resurrect these theories. That said, all hope is not lost for Neale's thesis. Davidson's highly influential theory, discussed in the next chapter, offers a way to treat quotations as quantified noun phrases (on the assumption that descriptions are quantifiers). It avoids, we will argue, most of the objections raised against the version of the description theory discussed in this chapter. It does, however, ultimately fail (so we will argue in sect. 10.4) because it ends up rendering quotation expressions context-sensitive.

10

The Demonstrative Theory

The seminal paper on quotation in the twentieth century is, almost by universal accord, Donald Davidson's 'Quotation' (1979).[1] It is without parallel the most discussed and influential paper on the subject. Davidson's view is alternatively called 'the Demonstrative Theory of Quotation' or 'the Paratactic Theory of Quotation'—both labels are well motivated, but we'll stick with the former. The Demonstrative Theory is presented in the final pages of 'Quotation'. The key passages are these:[2]

. . . quotation marks . . . help refer to a shape by pointing out something that has it . . . The singular term is the quotation marks, which may be read 'the expression a token of which is here'.

On my theory, which we may call the *demonstrative theory* of quotation, the inscription inside does not refer to anything at all, nor is it part of any expression that does. Rather it is the quotation marks that do all the referring, and they help to refer to a shape by pointing out something that has it.

Quotation marks could be warped so as to remove the quoted material from a sentence in which they play no semantic role. Thus instead of:

'Alice swooned' is a sentence

we could write:

Alice swooned. The expression of which this is a token is a sentence.

(*Ibid.* 90)

---

[1] This is not to say that Davidson's view is widely accepted, but only that it is the paper that most discussions of quotation center around. Versions of Davidson's view have been developed by Bennett (1988), García-Carpintero (1994), Cappelen and Lepore (1997b), Reimer (1996), etc.

[2] Similar views are intimated in Prior (1971: 60–1) and Christensen (1967); Partee (1973: 416–18) was also an early adherent. An interesting historical factoid: Davidson's paper was drafted in the 1960s and circulated among various philosophers and linguists. It is, for example, referenced in Partee (1973), some six years prior to its publication date.

So described, the Demonstrative Theory contains three central components:

(1) Quotation marks are treated as contributing a definite description containing a demonstrative to sentences in which they occur, i.e. the quotation marks in (1.4) become 'The expression of which this is a token', as in (10.1):

1.4. 'Bachelor' has eight letters.

10.1. Bachelor. The expression of which that is a token has eight letters.

Since Davidson (*ibid.* 85) takes expressions to be shapes or patterns, (10.1) is therefore equivalent to (10.2),

10.2. Bachelor. The shape of which this is a token has eight letters.

where an utterance of the second sentence is accompanied by a demonstration of an utterance of the first. According to Davidson, '. . . quotation marks . . . help refer to a shape by pointing out something that has it . . . The singular term is the quotation marks, which may be read 'the expression a token of which is here'' (*ibid.* 90). Davidson does not discuss direct quotation in his paper (which is somewhat odd since he does discuss mixed quotation), but extending Davidson's idea to direct quotation, (1.8) would be semantically construed as (10.3):

1.8. Quine said 'Quotation has a certain anomalous feature'.

10.3. Quine said (produced) a token of the pattern instantiated by that.

Quotation has a certain anomalous feature

where an utterance of the first sentence is accompanied by a demonstration of an utterance of the second.

(2) In the logical form of a sentence containing a quotation expression, whatever item occurs between the quotation marks in the surface syntax is discharged, so to speak, from the sentence containing that quotation. So, for any token of (1.4), whatever sits between the quotation marks in the surface syntax is not part of the sentence in which those quotation marks occur. It is demonstrated by that use of the quoting sentence.

(3) Utterances of quotation marks, by virtue of having a demonstrative ingredient, denote the expression instantiated by the demonstrated

token, i.e. the expression instantiated by the token that sits between the tokened quotation marks.

10.1. STRENGTHS OF THE DEMONSTRATIVE THEORY

The Demonstrative Theory is attractive for at least five reasons:

1. It explains opacity (D1): there's no reason to think that two sentences demonstrating different objects will take the same truth-value. Tokens of (1.4) and (1.5) demonstrate different objects, so there's no more reason to think that the move from (1.4) to (1.5) is truth preserving than there is to think that an inference from (10.4) to (10.5) is:

10.4. That's nice.

10.5. That's nice.

It's not that hard to imagine a speaker demonstrating distinct objects with these distinct utterances.

2. It obviously rules out quantifying in, since the quoted token is placed outside the quoting sentence, i.e. the Demonstrative Theory explains (D2).

3. To grasp the function of quotation marks is to acquire a capacity with infinite applications. The Demonstrative Theory explains why this is so: there's no limit on the kinds of entity that we can demonstrate. Hence, it explains (D3) without making quotation a productive device (for elaboration see Cappelen and Lepore 1997*b*). We can quote any quotable item whose tokens we can demonstrate.

4. There is no mystery about how to extend the vocabulary beyond the extant lexicon at any given time in the evolution of the language; since there's no limit to what can be demonstrated, there's no limit to what can be quoted. It thereby explains (D4). A sentence like

1.11. 'Snøman' isn't a word in English; it's a word of Norwegian.

can be true without extending the vocabulary of English one iota, because the item quoted by 'snøman' needn't be a part of English in order for (1.11) to be true; this item need only be something whose tokens can be demonstrated.

5. On mixed quotation, Davidson (*ibid.* 91) writes:

I said that for the demonstrative theory *the quoted material was no part, semantically, of the quoting sentence.* But this was stronger than necessary or desirable. The device of pointing can be used on whatever is in range of the pointer, and there is no reason why an inscription in active use can't be ostended in the process of mentioning an expression.   (our emphasis)

This, according to Davidson, is what goes on in (1.10). A token that is being used for one purpose is at the same time demonstrated for another: 'Any token may serve as target for the arrows of quotation, so in particular a quoting sentence may after all by chance contain a token with the shape needed for the purposes of quotation.' (*Ibid.* 90–1; cf. also Cappelen and Lepore 1997*b*) On this view, (1.10) is understood as (10.6):

> 10.6. Quine says, using words of which these are a token, that quotation has a certain anomalous feature.

(Here the 'these' is accompanied by a pointing to the token of Quine's words.) Thus, the theory offers an explanation of (D7).

10.2. WEAKNESSES OF THE DEMONSTRATIVE THEORY

Though (or maybe because) the Demonstrative Theory is both bold and radical, it has triggered an entire industry of criticism. Just about everyone writing on quotation since 1979 has attacked it.[3] We'll discuss only five of these objections. The first one can be rebuffed quite easily. The next two are more difficult to reply to, but we will propose tentative solutions on behalf of Davidson. They are tentative in the sense that we think ultimately even our recommendations succumb to the severe objections, of which there are two. The fact is that we see no way around these last two objections. These severe objections, indeed, have forced us to relinquish our prior commitment to the Demonstrative Theory (and to develop a new theory of quotation that we'll present over the course of Chs. 11–12).

---

[3] Some notable exceptions are Partee (1973), García-Carpintero (1994), and Cappelen and Lepore (1997*b*), though, alas, with this chapter we'll be switching to the side of the critics.

10.2.1. First Objection. The Problem of Open Quotation: Dangling Singular Terms

Recanati (2001) focuses on cases where quoted expressions do not serve as noun phrases in sentences. He has in mind cases like (8.2) and (8.3):

8.2. 'Comment allez vous?' That is how you would translate 'How do you do' in French.

8.3. Stop that John! 'Nobody likes me', 'I am miserable' . . . Don't you think you exaggerate a bit?

In these cases it looks like the Demonstrative Theory would have to postulate a dangling singular term, something like the nonsensical or ungrammatical (10.7) or (10.8):

10.7. That. Comment allez vous? That is how you would translate that in French. How do you do.

10.8. Stop that John. That. Nobody likes me. That. I am miserable. . . . Don't you think you exaggerate a bit?

In response to the counter-suggestion that (8.4) is not best represented by ungrammatical/unintelligible (10.8) but rather is elliptical for (10.9),

10.9. Stop that John! *You say* 'Nobody likes me', 'I am miserable' . . . Don't you think you exaggerate a bit?

Recanati (2001: 654) replies; 'I deny that [(8.3)] and [(10.9)] are synonymous. Nor are there any grounds for postulating ellipsis here except the desire to save the theory in the face of obvious counterexamples.'

10.2.1.1. Reply to Recanati

We can agree with Recanati that there is no grammatical evidence for treating (8.3) as syntactically elliptical for (10.9). But that need not be the counter-proposal. We doubt very much that any syntactician would want to treat (8.3) as a grammatical string in English. Yet we equally doubt that anyone would want to infer from this grammatical fact that an utterance of (8.3) is thereby prohibited from saying or conveying anything whatsoever. We (and we assume everyone else) believe that ungrammatical strings are used most (all?) of the time in order to express and convey information. The invocation of ellipsis in defending (10.9) as a paraphrase of an utterance of (8.3) needn't be any stronger than the claim that (8.3) can on occasion (maybe invariably in normal circumstances) be used to say (10.9).

Here's a simple test in defense of our claim. Imagine in a normal context after an utterance of (8.3) that someone tags on 'but he didn't say that John said it'. This addendum would make little sense.

10.2.2. Second Objection. The Problem of Relevant Features

According to Davidson, a quotation denotes an expression indirectly, by demonstrating a token that instantiates that expression. As we noted, Davidson (1979: 90) thinks that expressions are *shapes* or *patterns*. But then it is a problem for his view that any one token instantiates indefinitely many distinct shapes or patterns, and so, from his perspective, indefinitely many different expressions. You might worry, then, how on the Demonstrative Theory you could ever get from a particular token to a unique type, i.e. from a token to an expression.

Bennett formulates this problem thus:

Any displayed token has countless features, and so it is of countless different kinds. Therefore, to say

the inscription-types instantiated here: Sheep

or what amounts to the same thing,

the inscription-type each token of which is like this: Sheep

is to leave things open to an intolerable degree. How do we narrow it down? That is what I call the problem of relevant features. It urgently confronts the demonstrative theory which must be amplified so as to meet it. (Bennett 1988: 403, see also Washington 1992: 595–7)

Here's a related worry. Read (1.3) out loud.

1.3. 'The' is the definite article in English.

It seems obvious that your true spoken utterance of (1.3) says (makes) the same claim as the true typed token of (1.3) above. Yet, on the Demonstrative Theory at least, it remains unclear why this should be so: your spoken utterance demonstrates a vocal pattern and the typed one above a graphemic pattern. These two utterances, then, seem, on the Demonstrative Theory at least, to be attributing the same property to very different sorts of items. Intuitively, this result seems wrong.

10.2.2.1. Reply on Behalf of Davidson

Bennett (1988) considers two possible fixes:[4] Call them B1 and B2:

B1: A quotation refers to the largest (weakest) type every token of which resembles this:

    . . . in respects $R_1, R_2, . . ., R_n,$

with the displayed item—a token of the referent—in the gap [. . .] and with R's that are all and only the features that are linguistically significant in the language to which the displayed item belongs.   (Bennett 1988: 416–17)

B2: A quotation refers to the largest (weakest) type every token of which resembles the displayed item in all the respects that are significant in the language to which it belongs (*ibid*).

The difference between the two options is that B1 requires, while B2 does not, that the speaker know what the relevant features are. Proposal B2 instead defers that issue to 'the language to which [the displayed item] belongs'. Bennett provides one argument in favor of B1 and another argument in favor of B2; they run as follows.

Bennett's consideration in favor of B2 (*ibid*. 407) appeals to the intuition that we can understand a quotation even though we don't know what the relevant features of the quoted item are. Suppose you encounter (3.6):

3.6. '⩘' is a symbol used by Martians.

If it's your intuition that you can understand (3.6) without knowing what the relevant features of its quoted item are, then you should endorse B2. For according to B2, it is not a necessary condition on understanding a quotation that you know what the speaker takes to be the relevant features of the quoted item. All you need to know is that the quotation expression picks out whatever type it instantiates in the language to which it belongs (even for an unfamiliar language). If, on the other hand, you don't think that you can properly understand (3.6), then you should opt for B1.

Bennett provides some reason for this view in this passage (repeated from Ch. 3):

---

[4] Several suggestions are on offer for how to amend the Demonstrative Theory in this respect: cf. García-Carpintero (1994), Cappelen and Lepore (1997*b*, 1999*a*) and Davidson (1999).

If I don't know what features of inscriptions are significant in Martian, my grasp of any quotation of a Martian expression is essentially fragile. I can indeed extract information from it, but not in the way I do from quotations that I properly understand. Evidence for this: the only way I can safely pass the information along is by writing a perfect replica of the item my information displayed in his quotation, like the tailor who when told to copy a suit reproduced the tear in its sleeve. In other words, I can convey the information only by passing along my whole basis for it; and that shows that I am operating on something I don't really understand. (Bennett 1988: 407–8)

Bennett is not quite sure which considerations weigh the most here.[5] We appreciate his concerns, but just the same, in order to defend the Demonstrative Theory we believe the considerations in favor of the more restrictive B1 are stronger for the following reason.

Notice how peculiar Bennett's own set-up of his example is. Someone, not a Martian, utters a sentence employing an unfamiliar sign in a familiar language. This sentence (3.6) contains a quotation expression, and that expression includes unfamiliar marks between its quote marks. Suppose that the relevant features for individuating expressions in Martian are tastes and smells. If this were so, our intuition is that we, Cappelen and Lepore, speaking the language that we do, cannot use (3.6) to quote the Martian language. (In Ch. 12, we will develop a theory that has this as an implication.) Intuition is not our sole reason for being so inclined. We challenge anyone to find a single quotation expression used by a non-philosopher (outside scholarly work) where someone tries to quote smells or tastes. It just doesn't happen. That's evidence that we can't really quote Martian unless we have at least some way of picking out its relevant features. How this is best achieved, we will not speculate further upon here (though the issue will be pursued in Ch. 12). Even with these issues left unresolved, we think it is fair to say that the 'relevant features' objection might be answerable with a friendly amendment along the lines suggested by Bennett.

10.2.3. Third Objection: The Problem of Iteration

Recall, from Ch. 3, the problem of iteration. We pointed out there that a number of authors insist that a theory of quotation must explain why quotation satisfies (Iteration):

[5] Bennett (1988: 407–8) seems to be leaning in favor of B2, but he leaves the issue unsettled.

Iteration: The semantic value of an n-level quotation is a function (the result) of the semantic value of the corresponding n-1 level quotation being placed inside a pair of matching quote marks.

(where an n-level quotation is a quotation with n matching left and right quotation marks). The Demonstrative Theory obviously has difficulty in explaining iterated quotation, i.e. in satisfying (Iteration). The quotation expression (10.11), for example, refers to the quotation expression in (10.10):

10.10. 'smooth' is an English expression.
10.11. ''smooth'' is an English expression.

The Demonstrative Theory's account for (10.10) is (10.12).

10.12. Smooth. The expression of which that is a token is an English expression.

But how, then, can the theory accommodate (10.11)? (10.11), after all, includes two sets of quotation marks. Several authors have suggested that the Demonstrative Theory would then have to treat it as the ungrammatical (10.13) or the unintelligible (10.14) (cf. e.g. Saka 1998: 119–20, Reimer 1996, and Washington 1992).

10.13. Smooth. That that is an English expression.
10.14. Smooth. That. That is an English expression.

10.2.3.1. *Reply to the Iteration Objection*

In response, some proponents of Davidson's theory insist that quotations are not iterative. For example, Cappelen and Lepore (1997*b*: 439–40) say:

it does follow, on the demonstrative account, that quotation is not, contrary to a common view, genuinely iterative. Quoted expressions are exhibited so that speakers can talk about the patterns (according to Davidson) they instantiate. The semantic properties of the tokens are not in active use; they are semantically inert . . . So, quotation marks within quotation marks are semantically inert.

So far we are merely agreeing with Davidson's critics. How does any of this support Davidson? Our idea was this. Obviously, there is no upper bound on the length of expressions that can be quoted. However, it does *not* follow from this fact alone that quotation is a semantically *productive* device requiring a compositional semantic treatment. The argument for this is simple. Note that (10.15) is true.

10.15. ''F'' is not a quotation expression in Chinese.

It would seem that the truth of (10.15) requires that ''F'' can't refer, at least not as a matter of meaning alone, to a quotation expression. It would seem that the truth of (10.15) requires that it be semantically neutral on whether its quoted item is a quotation expression or not. If this is right, then its innermost set of quotation marks must be semantically idle. Hence, quotation marks would not be productive, and so, would not be iterative; and so the Demonstrative Theory would not be subject to this criticism. (We now think that this rejoinder is flawed in a very interesting way. We'll amplify on why in sect. 11.2 below.)

We turn to the severe objections against the Demonstrative Theory.

10.2.4. Fourth Objection: Too Much Context Sensitivity

The first severe objection should come as no surprise: According to the Demonstrative Theory, quotation marks are demonstratives. But demonstratives are context-sensitive expressions. Quotation expressions refer to whatever the speaker demonstrates (either through pointing or demonstrative intentions). If we take this idea seriously, though, then there's no guarantee, as a matter of meaning alone at least, that each utterance of, say, (1.4) will demonstrate the very same object.

Davidson insists that all these demonstratives demonstrate the pattern or the shape instantiated by the demonstrated token. But that's just *not* how demonstratives work. On the Demonstrative Theory, although quotations contribute the exact same meaning everywhere they occur, just the same they turn out to be context-sensitive. Which item gets quoted in any given context is always a function of whatever happens to be demonstrated or indexed in that context.

In Ch. 7, we argued that quotations are context-*in*sensitive. The arguments there naturally apply to the Demonstrative Theory inasmuch as it treats quotation expressions as context-sensitive. Recall, we presented two tests for context sensitivity: the Collectivity Test and the Inter-contextual Disquotational Indirect Reporting Test. Quotation, we argued in Ch. 7, fails both tests, and so it is not context-sensitive (in that connection we also appealed to Disquotation and the Proximity constraint; we elaborate on those objections below). Inasmuch as according to the Demonstrative Theory quotations *are* context-sensitive, that theory cannot be correct. So, we must relinquish commitment to the Demonstrative Theory.

10.2.4.1. *Reply on Behalf of Davidson*

We have been confronted with this objection to Davidson earlier; in particular, in an article by Stainton (who bases his argument on an objection in Burge (1986) to Davidson's paratactic theory of indirect speech). We have been inclined to respond as follows.

Davidson's theory can be salvaged by making a slight modification to the Demonstrative Theory, namely, by adopting an indexical instead of a demonstrative treatment of the quotation marks. Since for Davidson the logical form of (1.4) is (10.1),

> 1.4. 'Bachelor' has eight letters.
> 10.1. Bachelor. The expression of which that is a token has eight letters.

it's appropriate to ask for the character of the alleged demonstrative in (10.1). For example, according to Kaplan (1989), the character of 'I' is the speaker of the context; the character of 'now' is the time of the context; the character of 'today' is the day of the context; the character of 'yesterday' is the day before the day of the context. And so on. What, then, is the character for the word 'that' in (10.1)?

The context-sensitivity objection assumes that it's the standard one, namely, the demonstrated object of the context. But nothing in the Demonstrative Theory prevents us from positing as its character, instead, something like: *the type of the object placed between the quotation marks in the surface syntax of the sentence* (we can call it *the quotationally salient object*). Just as it's not an option to index someone else with your use of the first-person pronoun 'I'—no matter what your intentions are or which context you find yourself in—you also can't use a quotation to refer to anything other than the type instantiated by what's placed between the quotation marks. More precisely, the token surrounded by tokened quotation marks in a context of quotation must be the item that gets indexed on occasion of use. This amendment forces the speaker to refer to the type of the token in the sentence; and so this maneuver quiets the context-sensitivity objection. We build contextual stability into Davidson's theory by using the character of quotation marks to tie the referent to whatever is instantiated between the quotation marks in the surface syntax of the sentence. If this is an acceptable revision of Davidson's view, it would avoid the two objections to context-sensitive theories from Ch. 7.

10.2.4.2. Reply to the Reply on Behalf of Davidson

We no longer believe this modification is acceptable. The revised proposal is no longer a version of Davidson's theory: properly understood, it is not a demonstrative or indexical theory, and it is not a paratactic theory. There's nothing left of Davidson's proposal. What's left is too vague to constitute a genuine theory. We elaborate on these three points in turn:

a. The proposed revision doesn't treat quotation as the English demonstrative 'that' (because, on the revised proposal, quotation doesn't have the character of the English 'that', and that's essential to being the English 'that'). It in effect treats quotes as a new kind of term, call it 'Q', that designates the item quoted in the surface syntax of the sentence, i.e. the type (or expression) placed between the quotation marks in the surface syntax of the sentence containing the quotation marks (of course, in the logical form of the sentence, this material is placed outside the main sentence). Q is clearly not a demonstrative. Nor do we have any reason to treat it as an indexical because its semantic value in no way depends on extra-linguistic context. Its semantic value does not vary with context of utterance in the way the semantic value of other indexicals does. This is shown by the fact that, on the proposed revision of Davidson's view, no two utterances of a sentence S containing a quotation can ever differ in truth-value (assuming we keep the semantic values of other context-sensitive components stable). The semantic value of Q depends *only* on what's placed between the quotation marks in the surface syntax, and for any sentence, S, this will be the same for all utterances of S. Note that this dependency on what's placed between the quotation marks in the surface syntax is something that this proposal shares with all theories of quotation (except possibly the Proper Name Theory). So the distinctive feature of Davidson's theory, incorporating a demonstrative or indexical element, is removed from the revised version.

b. A Demonstrative Theory is one according to which the truth conditions of the main clause can be specified independently of the quoted material. Davidson (1979: 90) says, '. . . enough structure will be too much as long as we regard the quoted material as part of the semantically significant syntax of a sentence. The cure is therefore to give up this assumption.' The quoted material is expunged from the main sentence and the semantics for the main sentence can be specified without reference to it. This is another essential feature of

Davidson's proposal that's missing from the proposed revision. On the new proposal, a specification of the truth conditions for the main sentence includes a reference to the quoted material. The two are no longer independent, as they should be in a paratactic theory.

c. On the revised proposal, we're told that the quotation refers to 'the type' instantiated by the tokens placed between the quotation marks. That's not a uniquely identifying definite description. Indefinitely many types are instantiated by those tokens. So as it stands, this theory doesn't even begin to tell us how a quotation gets its semantic value.

In sum, Burge and Stainton were right: Davidson's theory postulates context sensitivity where there is none, and any attempt to bypass this problem relinquishes all that's distinctive about Davidson's theory.

It gets worse. This is not the *only* reason for rejecting Davidson's view. It surprises us[6] that we hadn't noticed sooner that, as a direct consequence of the Demonstrative Theory's commitment to context sensitivity, the theory cannot explain perhaps *the* most crucial and interesting feature of quotation: namely, its disquotational nature; nor can it explain the concomitant proximity feature connecting quotation expressions to what they quote. We turn directly to these objections.

10.2.5. Fifth Objection: Argument from Disquotation and Proximity

In Ch. 9, we rejected both the Proper Name and the Definite Description Theories partly because they failed to account for two indisputable features of quotation, namely, its disquotational nature, as exemplified in (7.7),

7.7. ' 'Quine' ' quotes 'Quine'.

and the proximity constraint on a quotation expression and what it quotes.

With regards to the former, ordinary speakers know that (7.7) is true simply by virtue of their competence with quotation, from merely

---

[6] Two research projects have occupied most of our joint philosophical attention during the past decade: the semantics of quotation (Cappelen and Lepore 1997*a*, 1998, 2005) and the limits of context sensitivity (1997*b*, 1999*b*, 2000, 2004). What we failed to notice is that our commitments with regards to the latter research program prohibit our commitments with regards to the former project. If you agree with us that the Indirect Disquotation Report and Collectivity Tests (and others) limit claims about (semantic) context sensitivity, then you must reject the Demonstrative Theory.

understanding the device of quotation. A theory of quotation, we insisted in Ch. 3, must guarantee that this obtains as a matter of meaning alone. But, of course, there can be no such guarantee on the Demonstrative Theory. For whether with an utterance of (7.7) the item demonstrated by a token of the first quotation quotes the item demonstrated by a token of the second quotation is an open empirical question. No matter how you choose to construe the idea of a truth obtaining as a matter of meaning, it should be clear that there's something fundamental about (7.7) that is not captured by such an account.

On a closely related point concerning the strong disquotational schema as manifested in (7.7), the Demonstrative Theory fares no better with respect to the proximity constraint on a quotation and what it quotes—its semantic value.

Just as with a proper name, the relationship between a demonstrative and what it demonstrates is arbitrary in this sense: the type instantiated by the item demonstrated or indexed with an utterance of a quotation is not included or contained in the quotation itself. Nor is there a backwards road from the token demonstrated to the expression type it instantiates. (It might after all instantiate an indefinite number of types.) Nor is the demonstration relationship a picturing relationship. This is particularly noteworthy since Davidson himself required that any adequate theory of quotation account for this picturing aspect of quotation. He says, '[the] theory must explain the sense in which a quotation *pictures what is referred to*, otherwise it will be inadequate to account for important uses of quotation, for example, to introduce novel pieces of notation and new alphabets' (Davidson 1979: 90; our emphasis). So, consider the quotation expression ' 'lobster' '. As noted in Ch. 9, it is not arbitrary that this quotation quotes what it quotes. In some sense, the expression 'lobster' is 'contained in' ' 'lobster' '. In some sense, ' 'lobster' ' pictures (or is an icon or hieroglyph of) 'lobster'. In some sense, we can go from knowing 'lobster' to knowing what its quotation is, and vice versa. But in a rather obvious sense, the Demonstrative Theory can't account for any of these features of quotation. It is certainly not a matter of language alone, that the expression a token of 'lobster' demonstrates must occur in the expression instantiated by a token of ' 'lobster' '. Furthermore, the pointing or demonstrating imagery that Davidson favors is not able to reconstruct the picturing one he himself requires of a theory of quotation.

10.3. CONCLUSION

In several articles over a ten-year period, we tried to show that Davidson's theory had more going for it than many of its critics had assumed. Seen in its historical context, Davidson's proposal is extraordinarily interesting and highly original. It took into account data that no other theory at the time could accommodate. It took the device of quotation more seriously than any other theory at the time did. The history of this subject matter is so closely tied to Davidson's view that practically all theories since then have been presented as alternatives to it. However, it is now time, we think, to leave that theory firmly behind. We admit we came late to this conclusion, but better late than never. The subject has moved to a point where we are much clearer on the totality of data and the relevant facts about syntax and semantics than, if we might modestly say, Davidson was. As a result, the Demonstrative Theory is no longer a useful starting point.

A theory of quotation should be an attempt to accommodate the extraordinary confusing array of data that we have gathered about our use of quotation throughout these pages. In the next chapter, we'll provide a theory of quotation that can, we hope, account for all of it.

11

The Minimal Theory

In Chs. 9–10, we argued against semantic theories that treat quotations as proper names, demonstratives, or quantifiers (in particular, as definite descriptions). In Ch. 8, we argued against pragmatic theories according to which quotations lack a semantic function altogether. So, then, what's left? The first moral we want to derive from this prior discussion is that, contrary to what you are led to believe by the entire history of the literature on quotation, theorists ought to take quotation dead seriously as a linguistic phenomenon. To this end, we presume that, unless doing so produces a catastrophe, quotation—like every other legitimate linguistic category—is ineliminable from a language without a loss of expressive power. No other linguistic category in our language can serve the complete function of quotation. This doesn't mean we lack ample resources for metalinguistic discourse in addition to quotation. We can name, describe, and demonstrate expressions; and we can also convey metalinguistic information pragmatically. But these practices, as we have argued over the course of this book, are not the same as quotation. With that consequence in mind, we turn to a semantic theory for quotation that celebrates its unique nature.

11.1. PRELIMINARIES: QS AND CONTAINMENT

Anyone not committed to the truth of (7.7) about the quotation expression ''Quine'' has a philosophical axe to grind:

7.7. ''Quine'' quotes 'Quine'.

As we noted in Ch. 3, the following disquotational schema for quotation is obviously correct:

(QS) ''e'' quotes 'e'

(where 'e' is replaceable by *any* quotable item[1]).

Instances of QS include not only (7.7) but infinitely many other sentences, including (11.1) and (11.2):

11.1. ''Quotation has a certain anomalous feature'' quotes 'Quotation has a certain anomalous feature'.

11.2. ''has a certain anomalous feature'' quotes 'has a certain anomalous feature'.

We proffer QS as *the* semantic rule for quotation. It serves as the full semantic treatment for quotation expressions. In other words, QS is the fundamental axiom schema governing the semantics of quotation expressions.

QS is the simplest, most natural, and most obvious semantic account for quotation expressions. It is indeed often presumed by various authors in passing, as if it were completely obvious. One version may be Richard's (1986: 397) DQR:

DQR: For any expression e, the left quote (lq) followed by e followed by the right quote (rq) denotes e.

We say 'may' because DQR uses 'denotes' where QS uses 'quotes' and it speaks of expressions rather than quotable items (the significance of which will emerge in Ch. 12), but the basic idea behind QS is already present in DQR.

Wallace (1972: 237) may also have QS in mind when he writes

. . . the denotation of the result of enclosing any thing in quotes is the thing itself.

QS seems also to be in Ludwig and Ray (1998: 163 n. 43); Mates (1972: 21); Salmon (1986: 6); Smullyan (1957); and Gomez-Torrente (2001: 145ff., 2005: 129). Each of these authors restricts the quotable items referenced in QS to expressions.

The Minimal Theory of Quotation (MT) is the view that QS is *the* semantic rule for quotation. It should be obvious that MT presumes a principle of Containment:

Containment: For any quotable item e, if a quotation expression Q quotes e, then e is contained in Q.

---

[1] In this chapter we will not tell you *what* a quotable item is. This chapter is mostly about the semantics of quotation and a little bit about its syntax. In Ch. 12, we say more about the nature of quotable items.

Containment describes a basic feature of quotation expressions. Though it will play no central role in the remainder of this chapter, its significance will become transparent in Ch. 12, where we will sketch a criterion for quotation expression individuation. The remainder of this chapter develops the semantic ramifications of MT in some detail; in particular, it aims to explain how MT is compatible with the practices of pure, direct, and mixed quotation.

11.2. MT AND ADEQUACY CONDITIONS (D1)–(D10)[2]

If someone asks how quotation functions in natural language, *the* obvious reply is something along the lines of QS. It is a pleasingly simple schema that requires no complicated assumptions about the surface structure of the sentences in which quotation expressions occur. The devil is always in the details, however. The rest of this chapter is largely devoted to showing how MT cooperates with the other relevant parts of a semantic theory; in particular, we aim to show how the semantic value of a quotation expression composes with the semantic values of other sorts of expressions with which it can grammatically combine productively. (In this regard, it turns out to be somewhat tricky to show how to explain mixed quotation; in particular, how to explain what we described in Ch. 3 as the syntactic chameleon nature of quotation.)

Before we begin, here's a preliminary overview of how MT fares so far against the adequacy conditions of Ch. 3. Some conditions will be deferred to Ch. 12 (since many of these adequacy conditions, we will argue, can be explained only after a viable theory of quotable items is available). But an initial progress report is very much in order.

Recall the adequacy conditions (D1)–(D10) from Ch. 3:

D1. Opacity
D2. Quantifying In
D3. Infinitude
D4. Extant Lexicon
D5. The Proximity Constraint and the Strong Disquotational Schema

---

[2] We argued in Chs. 4 and 5 that (D11) and (D12) are semantically irrelevant, and so they will not be discussed.

D6.   Syntactic Chameleonism
D7.   Simultaneous Use and Mention in Mixed Quotation
D8.   Indexicals Inside Mixed Quotation
D9.   Indeterminacy/Context Sensitivity/Ambiguity in Quotation
D10.   Iterability in Quotation

A viable theory of quotation should either explain each of (D1)–(D10)
or justify why an explanation isn't forthcoming.

(D1). Opacity. Can MT explain why we can't derive (1.5) from (1.4)
given that 'bachelor' and 'unmarried man' have the same semantic value?

   1.4. 'Bachelor' has eight letters.

   1.5. 'Unmarried man' has eight letters.

According to MT, the semantic values of ' 'bachelor' ' and ' 'unmarried
man' ' are the quotable items 'bachelor' and 'unmarried man', and not
the semantic values of these quotable items. The issue about opacity
therefore reduces to whether these two quotable items in (1.4) and (1.5)
are distinct. *Prima facie*, they certainly seem distinct, but in order to
back up this intuition a theory for how to individuate quotable items is
required, one that we will deliver in Ch. 12. (Looking ahead, we'll argue
that the semantic values of these two quotation expressions are different
simply because the expressions themselves are distinct.)

(D2). Quantifying In. Can MT explain why (3.1) can't be derived
from (1.4)? According to QS, what sits between the quotation marks in
(3.1) is a quotable item, and so ' 'x' ' quotes the quotable item 'x', thus
rendering the quantifier in (3.1) vacuous.

   1.4. 'Bachelor' has eight letters

   3.1. $(\exists x)('x'$ has eight letters).

(D3). Infinitude. QS tells us that any quotable item can be placed
inside its instances. Since there's no obvious *a priori* upper bound on
what quotable items are, there's no obvious upper bound on the number
of distinct quotation expressions. It is worth pausing here to point out
that it follows from the open-endedness of quotation that we have no
guarantee that the set of quotation expressions for a language can be
recursively generated. Postal (2004) holds that this fact about quotation
creates difficulties for standard views in syntax.

   The open-endedness of quotation rules out the view that there's a
finite list (be it an alphabet or some other list of features) from which the

expressions of natural language can be computed. From this fact, Postal draws dramatic conclusions about the nature of syntax and linguistic theory more generally. We won't discuss those alleged implications here (for further discussion, see Postal 2004; Lepore 1999) for that would take us too far afield from our main topic. What is certainly correct is that quotation requires a revision of the standard view according to which we are in the possession of a computational procedure that operates on items on a finite list.

However, from this it does not follow that a language with quotation contains infinitely many semantic primitives and is accordingly unlearnable. An expression is semantically primitive only if sentences in which it occurs cannot be understood on the basis of understanding sentences in which it does not occur. But on this characterization of a semantic primitive, distinct quotation expressions, according to QS, are *not* primitive. It is true that quotation marks are themselves semantically primitive—that's what the last four chapters led us to conclude—but from this it does not follow that quotation expressions formed with them are. Once identified, a sentence with a quotation expression can be understood without having to learn any new *semantic* fact (assuming one understands every other aspect of the sentence). That is, you can understand a quotation expression formed with quotation marks and an enclosed quotable item solely on the basis of understanding sentences in which that quotation expression does not occur.

(D4). *Extant Lexicon*. Quotation is not limited to an extant lexicon because the set of quotable items is unlimited. MT is, as a matter of fact, mute about what that set is. In Ch. 12, we'll argue that the set of quotable items contains items that are not themselves expressions in any language. Hence, the set of quotation expressions cannot be limited to an extant lexicon of any one language.

(D5). *The Proximity Constraint and the Strong Disquotational Schema*. This condition has three interconnected parts. It requires a theory of quotation to explain the proximity constraint (the particularly close relationship between a quotation expression and what it quotes), QS, and the strong disquotational nature of quotation, SDS, e.g. why only the quotation expression ' 'Quine' ' can quote the name 'Quine'. Since QS is the semantic rule governing quotation, it is not up for explanation (other than to say that it constitutes the semantic axiom schema for quotation). Proximity we get for free, so to speak, by virtue of MT's presumption of Containment. It remains to show how SDS follows from MT.

In Ch. 6, we argued that quotation expressions are neither context-sensitive nor indeterminate nor ambiguous. Combining these results with MT buys SDS. Here's an illustration:

- From QS it follows that for any quotable item e, ''e'' quotes 'e'. If ''e'' quotes some quotable other than 'e', say 'a', then it follows that the quotation expression ''e'' is ambiguous (because it quotes both 'e' and 'a').
- But, as we argued in Ch. 7, quotation expressions are unambiguous (and context-insensitive and not semantically indeterminate).
- So the quotation expression ''e'' can only quote 'e'.
- So SDS follows.

(D6). Syntactic Chameleonism. With respect to the syntactic chameleon nature of quotation, we will argue later in this chapter that MT is compatible with it. That is to say, we'll provide a grammatical account according to which the same quotation expression takes on different syntactic statuses in distinct linguistic environments (without changing its semantic value). For example, the quotation expression ''has a certain anomalous feature'' turns out to be in some contexts a noun phrase, and in other contexts a verb phrase. (That this is so will aid the effort to provide a viable semantics for mixed quotation sentences that respects QS.)

(D7). Simultaneous Use and Mention in Mixed Quotation. As we noted in Ch. 3, many authors, including a former time-slice of ourselves, claim that in (1.10) the quoted words are simultaneously used and mentioned.

1.10. Quine said that quotation 'has a certain anomalous feature.'

MT is *in*compatible with this intuition. However, the intuition itself is not robust, for as we noted in Ch. 6:

> When quotation marks in many mixed quotation sentences are removed, trouble ensues—in particular, in cases where the mixed quoted expressions contain indexicals, nonsense, or foreign expressions.

The remaining sections of this chapter, then, are for the most part devoted to explaining how we can relinquish this initial first-blush intuition behind (D7).

(D8). Indexicals Inside Mixed Quotation. Since MT denies that in mixed quotation sentences the quote expressions are both used and

mentioned (see (D7)), we automatically satisfy (D8), i.e. MT avoids the potential problem of claiming that a mixed quotation report implies the indirect quotation report that results from removing the quotes.

(D9). Indeterminacy/Context Sensitivity/Ambiguity in Quotation. We rejected (D9): we argued in Ch. 7 that quotations are context-insensitive. QS does not require the semantic context sensitivity of quotation expressions; hence, MT is consistent with the denial of (D9).

(D10). Iterability in Quotation. A number of authors argue that a theory of quotation must explain why quotation is iterable. According to QS, the semantic value of a quotation expression is a quotable item; indeed, it's the quotable item that that expression contains. This quotable item might be a linguistic expression or it might not be (more on this in Ch. 12). Suppose the quotable item is not a linguistic expression. Then, of course, it's not a quotation expression, and so, iterability is inapplicable. Suppose, however, that the quotable item is a linguistic expression. Then either that linguistic expression is itself a quotation expression or it is some other sort of expression. If it is not a quotation expression, then iterability, once again, does not apply to it. And even if it is a quotation expression, it might not be a quotation expression of English (but rather one of another language—we can quote quotation expressions from other languages), and so iterability does not apply to it. But suppose, finally, that the quotation expression that is contained within a quotation expression is itself an English quotation expression. Then, of course, QS applies to it and determines a semantic value for it—namely, its quotable item. In this regard, QS does not prohibit quotation expressions from being iterable. It's not clear what more we can ask of a semantic theory of quotation in this regard.

11.3. FURTHER DEVELOPMENTS: SYNTACTIC CHAMELEONISM AND MIXED QUOTATION

In earlier work, we rejected QS because it was incompatible with a feature we then believed held of mixed quotation (see e.g. Cappelen and Lepore 1997*b*; Lepore 1999). We were wrong: Mixed quotation lacks the feature we thought it had. One goal in this long section is to try to accommodate mixed quotation within the confines of a semantic theory that respects QS. Since quoted expressions are mentioned and not used in mixed quotation, we need to devise a semantics that allows a speaker to say something expressed by a clause that combines mentioned and used expressions. We will work our way up to a treatment of mixed quotation through discussions of the truth conditions for pure, direct, and indirect quotation.

11.3.1. THE ROLE OF QS IN A SEMANTIC THEORY

The role of QS in a compositional (interpretive) truth theory for English is to underwrite derivations of (interpretive) T-sentences like (11.3)–(11.5):

11.3. ''Bachelor' has eight letters' is true iff 'bachelor' has eight letters.

11.4. 'Quine said 'Quotation has a certain anomalous feature'' is true iff Quine said 'Quotation has a certain anomalous feature.'

11.5. 'Quine said that quotation 'has a certain anomalous feature'' is true iff Quine said that quotation 'has a certain anomalous feature.'

A semantic theory that aims to assign (interpretive) truth conditions but lacks (11.3)–(11.5) as consequences is woefully inadequate; and it should be equally obvious that a semantics that assigns propositions to pure and direct quotation sentences had better underwrite the propositional assignments (11.3.1)–(11.5.1):

11.3.1. ''Bachelor' has eight letters' expresses the proposition *that 'bachelor' has eight letters.*

11.4.1. 'Quine said 'Quotation has a certain anomalous feature'' expresses the proposition *that Quine said 'Quotation has a certain anomalous feature.'*

11.5.1. 'Quine said that quotation 'has a certain anomalous feature'' expresses the proposition *that Quine said that quotation 'has a certain anomalous feature.'*

We'll focus on the assignment of truth conditions as in (11.3)–(11.5) in this chapter (though what we have to say obviously extends to proposition talk); and so our question is how to supplement QS in order to derive these (interpretive) truth condition assignments. In this and the next two subsections we begin with pure and direct quotation sentences like (11.3) and (11.4) respectively, and later combine and exploit these two accounts in order to motivate one for mixed quotation sentences like (11.5).

11.3.2. PURE QUOTATION

How do we supplement QS in order to derive (interpretive) truth conditions for a pure quotation sentence like (1.4)? Assuming that its grammatical form is, roughly (with ' 'bachelor' ' a noun phrase (NP) and 'has eight letters' a verb phrase (VP)), something along the lines of

[NP VP]$_S$
1.4. 'Bachelor' has eight letters.

we introduce as relevant semantic axioms:

A sentence S of grammatical form [NP VP]$_s$ is true iff the semantic value of NP satisfies VP.
For any object x, x satisfies 'has eight letters' iff x has eight letters.

Using standard first order logic as well as these two semantic axioms (and the relevant instance of QS), we hope it's obvious how to derive (11.3):

11.3. ' 'Bachelor' has eight letters' is true iff 'bachelor' has eight letters.

11.3.3. DIRECT QUOTATION

Accommodating direct quotation sentences poses no further problems, *if* we make a not unreasonable assumption that their syntax is pretty much the same as that of pure quotation sentences. Assume[3] that the syntax of (1.8) is straightforward (with 'Quine' as its subject NP$_1$, 'said' as its main verb (V), and ' 'Quotation has a certain anomalous feature' ' as its grammatical direct object NP$_2$) along the lines of: [4]

[NP$_1$ [V NP$_2$]]$_{VP}$]$_S$
1.8. Quine said 'Quotation has a certain anomalous feature.'

---

[3] We assume that (since it's the subject) of (1.4) the quotation expression is an NP. There are reasons to challenge this assumption about *quotation expressions* in direct (and mixed) quotation sentences. We'll defend the view that a quotation expression can change its syntactic status without changing its semantic value across diverse linguistic environments below.

[4] In the appendix we'll try to improve upon this initial characterization of the syntax of direct quotation sentences.

A derivation (with obvious semantic rules) of the (interpretive) truth conditions for (1.8), then, runs along the lines of:

> 'Quine said 'Quotation has an anomalous feature'' is true iff <SV('Quine'), SV(' 'Quotation has an anomalous feature' ')> satisfies 'said'.[5]
>
> <SV('Quine'), SV(' 'Quotation has an anomalous feature' ')> satisfies 'said' iff Quine said 'Quotation has an anomalous feature'.

This account of direct quotation treats it pretty much like the one for pure quotation; and as with the latter, the semantic values of items inside the directly quoted 'Quotation has an anomalous feature' are semantically inert, and so irrelevant to the (interpretive) truth conditions of (1.8). It's as if these items, from a semantic perspective, are as Quine so forcefully pushed, not even constituents of (1.8). (The arguments for this treatment are in Ch. 6.)

It should be obvious how to extend the treatments of pure quotation sentence (1.4) and direct quotation (1.8) to derive (interpretive) truth conditions for endlessly other pure and direct quotation sentences. What's key is that looking over the derivations you can see that QS exhausts the full semantic contribution of quotation expressions to pure and direct quotation sentences.

With these treatments of pure and direct quotation in hand, we are just about positioned to present a semantic treatment of mixed quotation; still missing is a discussion—no matter how brief—of the semantics of indirect quotation.

11.3.4. INDIRECT QUOTATION

Anyone even only casually familiar with the literature on the semantics of indirect quotation knows that it is enormous; we cannot hope to do justice to all of it here. However, we need only say enough to motivate a treatment of mixed quotation. For this purpose, we'll go ahead and assume what is a perhaps customary and certainly a widespread view: namely, that the semantic value of a complement clause of an indirect quotation is a proposition or at least something proposition-like. In the case of (1.9), for example, we will assume for the purposes of this

---

[5] 'SV' stands here for 'the semantic value of'.

discussion that the proposition *that quotation has a certain anomalous feature* is the semantic value of the complement clause of (1.9).

1.9. Quine said that quotation has a certain anomalous feature.

(Other candidates include sentences, utterances, notions, and Interpreted Logical Forms (Larson and Ludlow 1993). Nothing relevant to our discussion about mixed quotation hangs on a choice here.)

On the assumption that the complement clauses of indirect quotations have propositions as their semantic values, we will further suppose, again for the purposes of this discussion, that the verb 'said' in indirect quotation expresses a relation between a speaker and this proposition. The indirect quotation (1.9), for example, is true, we will suppose, just in case Quine said the proposition *that quotation has a certain anomalous feature*.

We are finally ready to tackle mixed quotation along with its relations to these other forms of quotation.

11.3.5. SOME ADEQUACY CONDITIONS ON A SEMANTICS FOR MIXED QUOTATION

Mixed quotation is nothing if not an exceedingly complex phenomenon—one that requires us to account for an extraordinarily wide array of data. But the overarching goal has to be to explain how a quotation expression in the complement clause of a mixed quotation can syntactically *combine* with other linguistic expressions not quoted in that clause without sacrificing overall grammaticality; and then to show how the semantic value of that quotation expression (as determined by QS) semantically *composes* with the semantic value(s) of the other expressions in that clause in order to deliver a semantic interpretation for the entire complement, and ultimately, for the entire mixed quotation sentence. To these ends, we begin with a list of semantic *desiderata* on an adequate semantics for mixed quotation. (We do not mean to suggest that this list exhausts the semantic demands we can make of a theory of mixed quotation; it surely does not.) Semantic *desiderata* (DMQ1)–(DMQ4) should be familiar; each has been discussed in earlier chapters:

- **DMQ1.** Quotation expressions must respect QS everywhere they occur, including within a mixed quotation, and so, any adequate treatment of mixed quotation must be compatible with a semantically innocent account of quotation. In this regard, mixed quotation is required to be like pure quotation.

- **DMQ2.** Whatever proposition (if any) is expressed by the complement clause of a mixed quotation, quotations must not, once its quotation marks are removed, be assumed to be the proposition that is semantically expressed by the complement of that mixed quotation. That is, a proper semantic treatment of a mixed quotation sentence must *ensure* that its quoted items in its complement clause are *not used*. In this regard, mixed quotation is required to be like direct quotation.

- **DMQ3.** Any adequate account of a mixed quotation must ensure that the reported speaker said the quotable item quoted in the report (in order for the report to be true). In this regard, mixed quotation is again required to be like direct quotation.

- **DMQ4.** Any adequate semantic account of a mixed quotation sentence must ensure that the items not quoted in the report *are* used, and therefore, *do* make their normal semantic contributions. In this regard, mixed quotation is required to be like indirect quotation.

11.3.6. A SKETCH OF A SEMANTICS FOR MIXED QUOTATION

With these conditions in place, we can proceed to a sketch of a semantic treatment of mixed quotation. This treatment borrows from the above treatments for indirect and direct quotation. Its key ingredients are already in Cresswell and von Stechow (1982: 523), and derive from Richard (2005) (though they use a different formalism). Its development owes to John Hawthorne, Paul Pietroski, and especially Sam Cumming, each of whom has contributed to different stages of the account's development (though we concede that the account as things now stand remains far from complete).

We begin with two familiar intuitions: in direct quotation, the reported speaker is represented as saying a quotable item and in indirect quotation, the speaker is represented as saying a proposition (or something proposition-like—or at least this is the intuition of generations of semanticists working on the semantics of indirect quotation). The direct quotation sentence (1.8) is true just in case Quine said the quotable item 'Quotation has a certain anomalous feature'; and the indirect quotation sentence (1.9) is true just in case Quine said the proposition *that quotation has a certain anomalous feature*.

In mixed quotation, we are confronted with a seeming hybrid—a mixture of both direct and indirect quotation. Just as no one can say whatever is expressed by the complement of (1.9) without talking about quotation, so too no one can say whatever is semantically determined by the complement of (1.10) without discussing quotation. In this regard, the semantics of indirect and mixed quotation overlap. Moreover, just as the direct quotation (1.8) cannot be true without someone saying the quotable item 'Quotation has a certain anomalous feature', so too no one can say whatever corresponds to the complement of (1.10) without saying its quotable item 'has a certain anomalous feature.' In this regard, the semantics of direct and mixed quotation overlap.

Of course, there are ways in which mixed quotation is distinct from these other two forms of report: on the assumption—one strongly defended in this book—that the words quoted in (1.10) (much like those in (1.8)) are not used but only mentioned, the semantics of mixed quotation should not entail that whatever is semantically expressed by the complement of (1.10) is about a certain anomalous feature. In this regard, the semantics of mixed and indirect quotation are distinct. And, whereas the truth of (1.8) requires Quine to have tokened the word 'quotation', the truth of (1.10) does not; Quine may have designated quotation in all sorts of ways and still have said whatever (1.10) attributes to him. In this regard, the semantics of direct and mixed quotation are distinct.

Based on what we have said so far it is tempting to conclude that (1.10) is true just in case Quine said the quotable item 'has a certain anomalous feature' and spoke of quotation. But the account must go further. The truth of (1.10) requires Quine also to have predicated of quotation whatever corresponds to 'has a certain anomalous feature'. Or consider another example in (11.6):

11.6. Quine said that 'quotation' has a certain anomalous feature.

It's not enough to say that the truth of (11.6) requires Quine to have said the quotable item 'quotation' and spoken of having a certain anomalous feature. We need to guarantee that its truth requires Quine—to coin a phrase—to have *subjected* 'quotation' to having a certain anomalous feature.

In both the case of (1.10) and (11.6) the semantics must ensure that Quine tried[6] to apply the quoted expression in some manner or other to whatever non-linguistic materials are discussed in the mixed quotation.

---

6 See sect. 11.4 for why we say only 'tried.'

We can generalize this idea very roughly. A mixed quotation sentence of the form:

A said that F_1 Q F_2.

(where F_1 and/or F_2 are either empty or replaced by an appropriately used expression[7] and Q is replaced by an appropriate quotation) is true just in case A said $<Q; F_1, F_2>$. The saying relation obtains when the speaker A applied Q to whatever F1 and/or F2 discuss.[8]

Regardless of however complicated this semantic treatment may seem, its key idea is simple. Think of mixed quotation reports as affirming a saying relation between the reported speaker and an ordered pair: in the case of (1.10), the saying relation is between Quine and the ordered pair$<$'has a certain anomalous feature', [quotation ∂]$>$(where '[quotation ∂]' corresponds to, say, a propositional function which has quotation as its subject matter); in the case of (11.6), the saying relationship is between Quine and the ordered pair$<$'quotation', [∂ has a certain anomalous feature]$>$(where '[∂ has a certain anomalous feature]' corresponds to a propositional function which has *having a certain anomalous feature* as its predicative matter).

This account guarantees that no mixed quotation sentence can be true unless the reported speaker tried to apply that quoted item to the materials unquoted in the report.

11.3.7. TWO ADDITIONAL CONDITIONS ON AN ACCOUNT OF MIXED QUOTATION

Two further adequacy conditions on a treatment of mixed quotation revolve around the syntax of mixed quotation sentences (a topic about

---

[7] No more than one of F_1 or F_2 can be empty.

[8] To generalize, we need to consider cases of mixed quotation where more than one item is quoted in its report, as in 'John said that it was 'raining' when he 'left the party' '. These are commonplace. To this end, we need something more general roughly along the lines of:

A sentence of the form: A said that F_1 Q_1 F_2 . . . F_n Q_n

(where at least one F_i is replaced by an appropriately used expression and at least one Q_i is replaced by an appropriate quotation and the other F_j's are either empty or replaceable by the appropriately used expressions and the other Q_j's are either empty or replaceable by the appropriate quoted items) is true just in case: A said $< Q_1,...,Q_n; F_1,..., F_n >$. So, 'John said that it was 'raining' when he 'left the party' ' is true just in case John said $<$'raining'$_1$, 'left the party'$_2$; [it was ∂_1 when he ϕ_2]$>$—where subscripts indicate which place in the propositional function the quoted material corresponds to. More below in sect. 11.3.9.

which we have said next to nothing so far except for Searle's point in Ch. 6).

- **DMQ5**. Consider these parallel anaphora distributional data for indirect quotation (11.7) and mixed quotation (11.8).

  11.7. Mary said (that) Bill loves himself.
  11.8. Mary said (that) 'Bill' loves himself.

  According to our informants, both sentences are grammatically acceptable. Mary's uttering 'Bill loves himself' in normal circumstances not only renders (11.7) true, but, according to our informants, it also renders (11.8) true. (In this regard, Mary's uttering 'William loves himself' can render only (11.7) true, but not (11.8).)

  It would be surprising if whatever syntactic mechanisms are invoked to account for (11.7) don't also extend to the parallel (11.8).

- **DMQ6**. Consider these data concerning the linguistic phenomenon of VP-ellipsis. Both the indirect quotation (11.9) and the mixed quotation (11.10) are uniformly taken by our informants to be grammatical:

  11.9. Mary said that Bill loves himself and he does.
  11.10. Mary said that Bill 'loves himself' and he does.

- A standard syntactic treatment of VP-ellipsis for indirect quotation requires that the VP 'loves himself' be represented in the underlying syntax of the second conjunct and for deletion to occur in its derivation. In other words, at some level of linguistic analysis (11.9) would be represented as something like (11.9.1):

  11.9.1. Mary said that Bill loves himself and he does *love himself*.

  It would be surprising were this syntactic treatment of VP-ellipsis, if any good, did not to extend to mixed quotation. For this to be possible, in the relevant level of syntactic analysis for (11.10), the verb phrase 'loves himself' (not the quotable expression ' 'loves himself' ') must be represented in its second conjunct and deletion must occur on this represented verb phrase.[9]

---

[9] For a different account of similar data, see Benbaji (2005: 43–5). We reject his account because it assumes quotable items inside mixed quotations are used, something we argued against in Ch. 6.

11.3.8. (D6) SYNTACTIC CHAMELEONISM

The key to satisfying (DMQ5) and (DMQ6) lies with a solution we want to propose tentatively to explain the syntactic chameleon nature of mixed quotation discussed first in Ch. 3.

Since pure quotations are always NPs, it is tempting to extrapolate to the conclusion that all quotation expressions, wherever they occur are noun phrases (NPs), and so, that quotation expressions in both direct and mixed quotation sentences are NPs as well. This is a mistake. Though QS guarantees the semantic innocence of quotation expressions (the same semantic value being assigned to a quotation expression wherever it occurs), it is completely neutral on whether the syntactic properties of a quotation expression remain constant across linguistic contexts. The quotation expression ' 'has a certain anomalous feature' ', by virtue of being its grammatical subject, is an NP in (3.9),

3.9. 'has a certain anomalous feature' is not a complete sentence.

but it can't be one in (1.10), without flouting the obvious syntactic fact that it combines with an NP to form a clause. In this regard, as we noted earlier, quotation is a syntactic chameleon. To explain how this is possible, we suggest a simple rule for converting linguistic expressions of any grammatical category XP into quotation expressions of the same grammatical category. Consider the indirect quotation sentence (1.9):

1.9. Quine said that quotation has a certain anomalous feature.

In this sentence, the expression 'has a certain anomalous feature' is a VP that combines with the NP 'quotation' in order to form its complement clause. The rule we want to posit converts, so to speak, (1.9) into (1.10) through a function Q that maps linguistic expressions onto quotations of those expressions; Q maps 'has a certain anomalous feature' in (1.9) onto its quotation ' 'has a certain anomalous feature' ' in (1.10), while preserving its grammatical status.[10]

Slightly more formally, Q sits at the end of a node that sister-adjoins with another node. In the case of (1.10), it sits at the end of a node that sister-adjoins with a VP node; these two nodes together form a

---

[10] In this regard, in the grammar for English Q creates quotation expressions, though Q is not responsible for every quotation expression. Each quotation expression in a pure quotation, for example, is not generated by Q but rather, we'll assume, is generated directly in the lexicon.

VP node (which we'll conveniently label 'QVP'). The semantic value of QVP (a quotation expression) is determined by QS in its usual way. Since QS is indifferent to the grammatical status of the quotation expressions it interprets, it shouldn't matter what grammatical status a quotation has when QS is applied to it; it assigns the same semantic value (the same quotable item) to a quotation expression wherever it occurs—regardless of whether it is an NP in one context and a VP in another.

In (1.10), QVP corresponds to the quotation expression ''has a certain anomalous feature'' and its semantic value is the predicate expression 'has a certain anomalous feature'. Diagrammatically:

In general:

$$QXP \rightarrow Q\ XP$$

This rule enables us to accommodate the syntactic chameleon nature of quotation expressions.

11.3.9. ADEQUACY CONDITIONS (DMQ1)–(DMQ6)

The introduction of Q permits us in effect to align the accounts of indirect and mixed quotation by extending the shape of the account for indirect quotation to mixed quotation as well.

A semantic theory operates on syntactic/logical forms assigned to various sentences; semantic treatments must respect these assigned forms in deriving, say, interpretive truth conditions for any sentence. For an indirect quotation like (1.9), it is standard to assign a syntactic/logical form something along the lines of:

Indirect Quotation (IQ): $[NP_1 [V [C [NP_2 VP_2]_S]_{CP}]_{VP1}]_S$
1.9. Quine said that quotation has a certain anomalous feature.

IQ indicates that the main verb 'said' of (1.9) takes not an NP as its grammatical object (as we assumed above for the grammar of direct quotation), but rather a complement clause CP. C corresponds to a complementizer, in this case 'that' (sometimes null, as in 'Quine said quotation has a certain anomalous feature'). Likewise, for mixed quotation sentences like (1.10), we will posit a syntactic form along the lines of:

> *Mixed Quotation Surface Form* (MQSF):[11] [NP$_1$ [V [C [NP$_2$ [Q VP$_2$]$_{QVP}$]$_S$]$_{CP}$]$_{VP1}$]$_S$

It should be clear that MQSF is motivated by the grammatical similarity between mixed and indirect quotation. Both IQ and MQSF take complement clauses CP. The key difference is Q. Q in MQSF sister-adjoins with a node, in this case a VP, to form a new VP (labeled 'QVP'). In (1.10), QVP corresponds to the quotation expression ' 'has a certain anomalous feature'' and its semantic value is the quotable item 'has a certain anomalous feature', which according to MQSF is a VP.

In MQSF, QVP is inside the CP; however, in the logical form of (1.10), we'll assume QVP raises to its head CP, leaving a trace t behind, something along the lines of:

> *Mixed Quotation Logical Form* (MQLF): [NP$_1$ [V [[Q VP$_2$]$_{QVP(t)}$ [C [NP$_2$ [t]$_{VP_2}$]$_S$]$_{CP_1}$]$_{CP_2}$]$_S$

Diagrammatically, its complement clause looks like this:

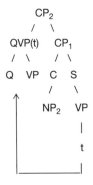

We hope that you can see, even with only this sketch of the syntax, that this account of mixed quotation provides a compositional semantics, accommodating (DMQ1)–(DMQ4), and it also accommodates syntactic constraints (DMQ5) and (DMQ6).

---

[11] Of course, this form has its VP mixed quoted; different forms will correspond to sentences with other grammatical components mixed quoted.

With regards to (DMQ5), (11.8) is grammatical because its QNP 'Bill' leaves a trace t that c-commands 'himself' and co-indexes with it.

11.8. Mary said (that) 'Bill' loves himself.

And we can tell a similar story for (11.10):

11.10. Mary said that Bill 'loves himself' and he does.

Since ' 'loves himself' ' is a QVP that has 'love himself' as its constituent VP, whatever the story is about the well-formedness of (11.9) extends to (11.10).

We hope it is also clear why this treatment accommodates (DMQ1)–(DMQ4).

Condition (DMQ1) is met because QS holds for quotation expressions in mixed quotations no less than for those in pure and direct quotation. The semantic value of ' 'a certain anomalous feature' ' is the same wherever it occurs; the application of Q together with raising the quotation permits us to respect QS.

Condition (DMQ2) is also accommodated. Quoted materials in a mixed quotation are not used if by that it is meant that a mixed quotation semantically expresses the same proposition as its quotationless indirect quotation counterpart. As a result, the quoted material in a mixed quotation does not contribute standard semantic values to the propositions expressed by that clause; again raising permits us to do this.

Condition (DMQ3) is satisfied because if an expression is mentioned (quoted) in the complement of a mixed quotation sentence it will raise to the first member of the pair said. This, given the semantics, guarantees that a mixed quotation cannot be true unless its quotation expression was said.

Condition (DMQ4) is satisfied since the account guarantees that the structures used in the complement clause of a mixed quotation contribute to the structure and content of the propositional function determined by that complement.

Of course, none of these observations are substitutes for a detailed analysis.

In summary: we believe the account of mixed quotation can explain, in an intuitive way, the data and adequacy conditions placed on it—both syntactic and semantic; both those peculiar to mixed quotation and those requiring a semantic and/or syntactic overlap among direct, indirect, and mixed quotation. We turn now to some residual problems.

11.4. GIBBERISH, FOREIGN EXPRESSIONS, AND INDEXICALS

Given the current treatment of mixed quotation, we can return to the puzzling data from Ch. 6 involving the behavior and legitimacy of nonsense words, foreign expressions, and indexicals in mixed quotations. This treatment will interpret $(C2^\wedge)$, (6.4), and (6.8) respectively as something along the lines of $(C2^\wedge)_{Int}$, $(6.4)_{Int}$ and $(6.8)_{Int}$:

> $(C2^\wedge)$ He says that it will have 'a more elegant, refined taste than the one I'm making now.' (Indexical inside the mixed quote.)
> 6.4. Nicola said that Alice is a 'philtosopher'. (Gibberish inside the mixed quote.)
> 6.8. Galileo said that the earth 'si muove'. (Foreign words inside the mixed quote.)
> $(C2^\wedge)_{Int}$ He says $<$'a more elegant refined taste than one the one I'm making now', [it will have t]$>$
> $(6.4)_{Int}$ Nicola said $<$'philtosopher', [Alice is a t]$>$
> $(6.8)_{Int}$ Galileo said $<$'si muove', [the earth t]$>$

Key to understanding these three interpretations are:

> $(C2^\wedge)_{Int}$ is neutral about *whom* the reported speaker of $(C2^\wedge)$ is indexing with his utterance of 'I'.
> $(6.4)_{Int}$ is neutral about *what* Nicola was attributing to Alice with her utterance of 'philtosopher'.
> $(6.8)_{Int}$ is neutral about *what* Galileo was predicating of the Earth with his utterance of 'si muove'.

This silence is exactly as it should be. Understanding English does not enable its practitioners to know what if anything Nicola said Alice was or what Galileo predicated of the Earth; and furthermore, on the basis of understanding indexicals *alone* English speakers do not know whom the reported speaker indexed.

Of course, none of this means that speakers can't be reliable judges about what was going on in those original contexts of utterance. Audiences draw all sorts of conclusions on the basis of hearing an utterance, including a mixed quotation one—conclusions often not underwritten by the semantics, but rather on the basis of reasonable assumptions about the reported speaker. For example, since he was speaking English and, as a matter of meaning, a use of 'I' picks out its user, whoever he is, given (C2^) we can reasonably infer that that use of 'I' picks out the reported speaker himself.

Based, however, on competence with the English word 'now', though we know that when he spoke he was picking out the time of his utterance, we don't know which time that is. We can describe it—based on competence with 'now' alone—but we can't refer to it. The same goes for demonstrative expressions.

When someone tells us (11.11),

11.11. John said that he was never going to like 'that man'.

we are in no position to *demonstrate* the man John's reported utterance demonstrated (if any), but we can *describe* that individual (based on an understanding of the words mentioned in the mixed quotation) as whichever man John demonstrated with his original usage.

With foreign expressions and gibberish, since we ourselves don't speak Italian or recognize 'philtosopher', there is nothing to do as a matter of linguistic competence except to describe the speaker as having said something expressed (if anything) with the words in question.

With (1.10) we can of course go further than we can with linguistic expressions we neither understand nor are familiar with since 'has a certain anomalous feature' is English and we understand English. Recall that according to QS, we cannot grasp a quotation expression without grasping its quotable item (inasmuch as it is a constituent of the quotation). So competence with English alone enables us to recognize that English expressions are being quoted in (1.10) and also what those words mean. This is what enables us to infer that the reported speaker of (1.10) is telling us that Quine said that quotation has a certain anomalous feature.

11.5. CONCLUSION

This chapter has been both ambitious and incomplete. We have not done more than sketch an account of mixed quotation and a lot more would need to be said to show that the account is complete.[12] However,

---

[12] For example, on the current account only well-formed expressions can be mixed quoted. But the data on that is mixed. Is there anything wrong with 'John said that 'Bill left' his mother at home'? If not, then the current account would need to be modified to accommodate such data.

if this account is right (and we believe it or something close to it is), then almost everyone who has ever written on mixed quotation since Davidson (1979), including ourselves, has been confused and mistaken.

What remains to be explained is how to reconcile QS with the strong disquotation principle SDS and the proximity constraint from Ch. 3. Accounting for these features is the most important task confronting a theory of quotation, for these features distinguish quotation as a linguistic phenomenon from every other one in natural language. They are what afford quotation its special place in the linguistic taxonomy. We turn to these important topics in the next and final chapter.

Direct Quotation—a Second Run

We succeeded in assigning an overlapping syntactic/logical form to indirect and mixed quotation. But we assigned to direct quotation a very distinct syntactic/logical form. This came about from the assumption prevalent throughout the literature that in direct quotation the quotation expression is a noun phrase (see e.g. Simchen 1999: 326, and Saka 1998: 120, 127). But anomalies in this treatment of direct quotation urge a more complicated and subtle treatment.[13]

Recall from Ch. 3, for example, the occurrence of 'has a certain anomalous feature' in (3.10):

3.10. Quine said 'has a certain anomalous feature'.

If 'said' is a transitive verb, then its direct object ''has a certain anomalous feature'' is a noun phrase, but on second glance, the grammar of (3.10) seems more complicated. Ordinary transitive verbs like, say, 'boils,' do not permit substitution of their direct object for their subject while preserving meaning. Examples (3.11) and (3.12), though grammatical, are not synonymous.

3.11. John boiled the water.
3.12. The water boiled John.

But we can exchange the quotation expression in (3.10) with its subject without a change in meaning. Examples (3.10) and (3.13) are synonymous:

3.13. 'has a certain anomalous feature' said Quine.

This data suggests a more complicated story about the syntactic status of quotations in direct quotations than the one we gave in the chapter.

Furthermore, various data adduced for treating mixed and indirect quotation sentences as syntactically akin seem to extend to direct quotation as well. Recall the data from Ch. 3: namely, that in (11.12)

11.12. Jones said 'Smith rules the moon', and he does.

''he' picks up Smith as its referent instead of the word 'Smith'' (Seymour 1996: 309). Or consider this other example from Partee (1973: 412):

11.13. The sign says 'George Washington slept here' but I don't believe he really ever did.

---

[13] This appendix has benefited from the discussions of the syntactic and semantic complexities of direct quotation in Partee (1973), Cram (1978), and Munro (1982).

An account for direct quotation, if possible, should account for the anaphora relationships between 'he' and 'Smith' in (11.13) and 'George Washington' and 'he' in (11.13). They seem no less grammatical or interpretable than (11.9) and (11.10).

11.9. Mary said that Bill loves himself and he does.
11.10. Mary said that Bill 'loves himself' and he does.

The 'he' in each of these seems to be picking up on whatever 'Bill' or 'Smith' or 'George Washington' picks out respectively. If this is right, then it would seem to be a presupposition of (11.12) and (11.13) that 'Smith' and 'George Washington' pick someone out. Furthermore, the 'does' ('did') would seem to represent a VP deletion of 'rules the moon' in (11.12) and 'slept here' in (11.13).

Reading more structure into direct quotation sentences than we have so far acknowledged would enable us to account for these various sorts of linguistic data. It may be that we cannot treat direct quotations as NPs. That is, to the extent that these various data are acceptable, there is a greater demand for a uniform syntactic treatment of indirect, mixed, *and* direct quotation.

Pulling all these different strains together, we want to posit a more complicated syntactic/logical form for direct quotation sentences—something along the lines of:

Direct Quotation (DQ): $[NP_1 [V [[Q [NP_2 VP_2]s]_{QS}]_{CP}]_{VP1}]s$

Q is familiar; in this case it sister adjoins with S to form a QS. DQ suggests the following semantic derivation for (1.8):

'Quine said 'quotation has a certain anomalous feature'' is true iff <SV'Quine', <SV' 'quotation has a certain anomalous feature'', Ø> satisfies 'said' iff Quine said <'quotation has a certain anomalous feature', Ø>

(where 'SV' stands for 'semantic value'). Unlike with mixed quotation sentences, the second member of the ordered pair satisfying 'said' in direct quotation is null. The speaker with a direct quotation, as a matter of meaning alone, does not commit himself in the direct quotation itself to how the non-linguistic matters stand. He's said nothing about the non-linguistic world with his direct quotation. In this regard, with direct quotation, the semantic properties of a directly quoted expression (if any) are rendered semantically inert by Q for the purposes of evaluating a direct quotation sentence. However, inasmuch as the expressions within the direct quotation are still in the underlying form of the sentence, the standard syntactic stories, whatever they may be, can still apply to them—in order to account for, e.g., linguistic data about anaphora and VP-ellipsis.

12

On the Nature of Quotable Items: Signs and Expressions

According to the Minimal Theory, a quotation expression quotes whatever quotable item it contains; accordingly, ''bachelor'' quotes 'bachelor'. Not surprisingly, the theory is mute about the nature of its semantic values, i.e. it is mute about what the quotable item 'bachelor' is. This is as it should be, since it's not the role of a semantic theory to inform us about the nature of the things we talk about. Semantics is not metaphysics, physics, biology, psychology or, etc. Just the same, an account of the nature of quotable items is needed in order to determine what quotation expressions themselves are. That is to say, without a story about the nature of quotable items, we'll argue, we can't know which expressions the Minimal Theory applies to. A happy consequence of this account will be a viable *non*-semantic, *non*-pragmatic treatment of the recalcitrant variability data that thwarted us in Ch. 7.

The chapter proceeds as follow: In sect. 12.1. we introduce an obvious (though surprisingly overlooked) distinction between signs and expressions and invoke this distinction and the Minimal Theory of Ch. 11 to underwrite an account of quotation expression individuation. In sect. 12.2, we exploit this account of quotation expression individuation in order to explain (away) the recalcitrant variability data from Ch. 7. In sect. 12.3, we explain why so many authors (and speakers) are misled into thinking a single quotation expression can be used to pick out distinct quotable items on different occasions.

12.1. SIGNS AND EXPRESSIONS

We begin with the obvious: different media can be used to articulate the same message. We can *write* English on a piece of paper; we can *speak* it out loud with different pronunciations; we can *type* it with the Roman alphabet (in indefinitely many fonts and sizes), in italics, in bold, in Braille, in Morse code; we can *sign* it with finger gestures or *wave* it in semaphore. These constitute but a tiny fragment of indefinitely many distinct ways in which we can articulate the same language and the same expressions to get across the same message. Call each a *sign system for articulating English.*

New sign systems are constantly emerging or evolving. A case in point is the novel system of blinks that Stephen Hawking uses to articulate English. The British physicist is the long-term survivor of the debilitating Motor Neurone disease. He has been using one hand to control a computer which gives him a voice, but as his hand weakens he uses a gadget which allows him to control the computer by eye blinks. The fact is that only our imaginations limit the number of distinct sign systems that could be employed in articulating natural language.

What's key in this discussion is that languages and sign systems are distinct so that no language is essentially tied to any particular sign system or even to any set of sign systems. It might be that for most natural language users spoken sign systems take on more practical significance than other sorts of sign systems; however, if as a result of a global catastrophe the human race went mute, you could still read this sentence, and you would be reading an English sentence. You could still write or record or even sign a reply to it, and that reply could also be in English.

Since no sign system is essential for the continued existence of any natural language, speakers who do not share a sign system might still share a language. Consider A, B, and C. A speaks, but is illiterate (i.e. does not read or write). B is deaf/mute and only reads and writes. C is blind and deaf and only communicates in Braille. A, B, and C can all be English speakers, even though they are incapable of communicating for lack of a common sign system.

In the other direction, people who share a sign system may still not be able to communicate since they do not share a language. From time to time, the Norwegian half of this collaboration sends emails to the American half using the same signs that the latter uses in replying. It's convenient to use the same sign system; indeed, our common computer keyboards and software insist upon it. But were the Norwegian to use this common sign system to articulate Norwegian, it would not facilitate communication since the American understands not a word of Norwegian.

12.1.1. A Philosophical Theory of Sign Systems

That signs exist is uncontroversial; but how best to individuate them is another story. Are items in different fonts different signs? What about differences in font size? Do all handwritings constitute different sign systems? What about different pronunciation patterns? We will not attempt to answer these interesting questions here; we are quite sure they are not primarily philosophical. They are the subject matter of entire disciplines: phonology, phonetics, graphology, etc., and it not clear what we as philosophers can contribute to this debate beyond the general remarks presented above. It's an empirical question how to classify signs, what their distinctive features are, and how they are processed, produced, and mentally represented. For our purposes, the only point that needs emphasis is that signs (no matter how they are characterized and individuated) are distinct from expressions: expressions are not bound to any particular sign system whereas signs obviously are, and signs are not bound to any language whereas expressions are. Once made, these two points, no matter how obvious, are regularly missed or flouted primarily because the distinction between signs and expressions itself is often missed or flouted. What, however, does this distinction have to do with the explicit aim in this chapter, namely, individuating quotation expressions? We turn to this question directly.

12.1.2. What Are the Quotable Items?

Quotations are expressions in natural language; otherwise, they could not be legitimate constituents of sentences of these languages. As with any expression type, a quotation expression when articulated must be articulated with a sign. That should be uncontroversial. Signs, as with any other kind of entity, can be named, described, or demonstrated; and once picked out, various attributes can be ascribed to them. We might discover a particular sign used in articulating different expressions in one or many languages—expressions that differ in meaning, and so on and so forth. These, we presume, are also uncontroversial points.

We hope it is no less obvious that in addition to being namable, describable, and demonstrable, signs are quotable, as in (12.1).

12.1. 'Red' is a sign that articulates one word in English and a different word in Norwegian.

According to (12.1), one and the same sign is used to articulate distinct words (in different languages). Example (12.1) requires for its truth that its quotation expression (its grammatical subject) has as its semantic value, that is, has as whatever item it quotes, a sign. The semantic value of the subject of (12.1) is not two words but rather a single sign.

In addition to signs, expressions are also quotable items, as in (12.2):

12.2. 'Red' is an English word.

Notice that we can say of the word quoted in (12.2) that in our spoken sign system it's pronounced in exactly the same way as the word 'read' is. So distinct graphic signs can be used to articulate different words, but, because of a historical accident, the same spoken sign can be used to articulate both. Again, we presume, this is obvious.[1]

In sum: differences between (12.1.) and (12.2.) indicate that quotation expressions can quote distinct kinds of items. What's quoted in (12.2.) is from a certain language (English); it has a certain meaning. What's quoted in (12.1.) is not, nor does it have meaning.

Signs in general are not language-specific and lack meaning (except possibly in some derivative sense). We don't infer that the word 'red' is ambiguous because two words with distinct meanings can be pronounced in the same way (i.e. with the same spoken sign).[2]

12.1.3. Containment

Since both signs and expressions are quotable, it follows that if, as we established in Ch. 7, a quotation expression is neither ambiguous nor context sensitive nor semantically indeterminate, then if it quotes an expression it cannot be quoting a sign, and if it quotes a sign it cannot be quoting an expression. On this view, (12.3) and (12.4) might both be true.

---

[1] The distinction between signs and expressions in the quotation literature goes back at least to Linsky (1950) and perhaps also to Reichenbach (1947). It is also exploited and discussed in Cappelen (1999) and Cappelen and Dever (2001). It does raise interesting questions about what sort of objects expressions are. We will not try to present a metaphysical theory of expressions. Suffice it to say that any linguistic theory has to recognize such entities and we will leave it for others to characterize them in detail. What is clear is that the same expression can be both e.g. spoken and written. As a result, they must be distinct from signs. This principled distinction is all we need for the purposes of this chapter.

[2] Looking ahead, that we are committed to there being different sorts of quotable items—signs *and* expressions—doesn't distinguish us from anyone who endorses QCS from Ch. 7: variability *only* makes sense on the assumption that a single quotation expression can be used to quote distinct quotable items.

12.3. 'Red' is a sign and not an expression.

12.4. 'Red' is an expression and not a sign.

If (12.3.) is true, its grammatical subject quotes a sign, and if (12.4.) is true, its grammatical subject quotes an expression. How, given the critical arguments of Ch. 7, can we explain this possibility? That is, given that quotation expressions are not semantically context-sensitive/ ambiguous/indeterminate, how can both (12.3.) and (12.4.) be true?

According to the Minimal Theory, quotation expressions *contain* as constituents their semantic values—namely, quotable items are constituents of the quotation expressions that quote them. Although we initially spoke of containment in somewhat metaphorical terms, it should be clear from Ch. 11 that we intend it quite literally.[3] But if quotation expressions contain what they quote as constituents, it follows that if a quotation expression quotes a sign, then that sign must be a constituent of that quotation expression; and if it quotes an expression, then that expression must be a constituent of that quotation expression. In short, two quotation-expressions are distinct just in case they disagree in semantic value (or much the same, just in case they don't share identical constituents).

12.2. SOLUTION TO THE PUZZLE ABOUT QUOTATION

With these general comments in place, we have positioned ourselves nicely to explain (away) the recalcitrant variability data about quotation from Ch. 7. The explanation is peculiarly syntactic, based on the account of quotation expression individuation from sect. 12.1.

12.2.1. Recalcitrant Data Revisited

In Ch. 7, we argued that quotational variability could not be explained by invoking semantic context sensitivity. Any such effort, we argued, fails on several counts:

1. It can't account for the status of SDS.

(SDS) Only ' 'e' ' quotes 'e'

---

[3] The sense of 'containment' we have in mind here is intended to be no less innocent than its sense when we say of a sentence that it contains any number of expressions.

(where 'e' is replaceable by any quotable item whatsoever).
2. It can't account for the proximity relation.
3. It fails the collectivity and disquotational indirect reporting tests for (semantic) context sensitivity.

However, we ended Ch. 7 by discussing variability cases that seem to pass these two tests. That is to say, we ended that chapter confounded inasmuch as earlier in that same chapter we presented convincing quotation cases that obviously failed these same tests. We return to these puzzling cases in what follows because we believe they clarify the significance of quotation expression individuation in providing their own explanation.

Recall (7.6.1):

7.6.1. 'Madrid' = 'Madrid'

Times Roman is used on the left and side, and Verdana on the right (in different font sizes). Again, first, imagine (7.6.1) tokened in a context C where the speaker is typing a rather obvious identity, but mid-sentence some strange formatting key is unintentionally pressed on the computer and switches font from Times Roman to Verdana (and where the font makes no difference to the writer at all—she doesn't know what font she's writing in, doesn't know it changed mid-sentence, and wouldn't have cared if she did notice). Intuition is that the resulting utterance is true. Next imagine (7.6.1) tokened in a context C' where the writer is intending to bring to her audience's attention the differences between the Times Roman and Verdana. She might utter (7.6.1) as a test case to her audience. In this context it's easy to get the intuition that (7.6.1) is false and (7.14) true:

7.14. 'Madrid' ≠ 'Madrid'

As noted in Ch. 7, this seems to show that in some cases quotation expressions pass the tests for semantic-context insensitivity. We have found ourselves in a most unfortunate position—for we seem to have produced cases of quotational usage that show that quotation expressions do not pass the tests for semantic-context sensitivity; and other cases where quotation expressions do pass these same tests. How can that be? What we need, and what has been transparently missing in the discussion so far, is an account of how quotation expressions are to be individuated. We turn to that task next.

12.2.2. Recalcitrant Data Explained Away

First notice that any theorist who endorses either a semantic *or* a pragmatic explanation of any quotation variability data must assume that concomitant intuitions are about distinct utterances of the very *same* quotation expression. This is the assumption we will directly challenge (at least in some cases) in what follows. Doing so requires answering two questions:

Q1: How could the utterances in question be of different quotation expressions?
Q2: Why have theorists and informants tended to believe otherwise?

We begin with (Q1).

How can we even discuss the recalcitrant variability data without assuming expression type-identity across contexts of utterance? Our answer is simple.

We concluded in sect. 12.1.3. that since both signs and expressions are quotable, if a quotation expression quotes an expression, it cannot be quoting a sign and if it quotes a sign, it cannot be quoting an expression. The relevance of these claims *contra* semantic context sensitivity should be clear. Tests for discerning semantic-context sensitivity—e.g. the Indirect Disquotational Reporting and the Collectivity Tests—presume linguistic stability—by which we mean they presume that what's indirectly disquotationally reported or collected are the same expressions as those originally tokened. Pragmatic strategies for explaining intuitions about quotational variability also presume linguistic stability; each assumes that the same quotation sentence might convey different propositions in different contexts. However, on the current proposal for individuating quotation expressions, failure to collect, for example, (7.6.1) and (7.14) into (7.15) results from a *syntactic* and not a *semantic* equivocation. For the imagined true utterances, the subject of (7.14) is not the same expression as the subject of (7.6.1):

7.6.1. 'Madrid' = 'Madrid'
7.14. 'Madrid' ≠ 'Madrid'
7.15. 'Madrid' = 'Madrid' and 'Madrid' ≠ 'Madrid'

And since their grammatical subjects are not the same, neither are their subject matters, and so trying to collect them into a single sentence is as confused as trying to collect expressions from different languages into a single sentence in a single language. No one would conclude an English word is ambiguous or semantically context-sensitive because a sign that articulates it in English also articulates other words from other languages with different meanings.

The same point extends to the other test. An indirect disquotational report of a true token corresponding to the non-identity in (7.14) would fail were it spoken because spoken signs are distinct from written ones, and so *if it's signs that are being quoted* then obviously the one medium cannot be utilized in reporting the other—since the medium itself provides the subject matter of this quotation sentence.[4] However, an indirect disquotational report of a token corresponding to the true identity in (7.6.1) can succeed when the quoted items are the same word, and not distinct signs.

Since both semantic and pragmatic context sensitivity presume the same expression is being indirectly disquoted or collected, and since, on the current proposal, this presumption is not true for all cases of quotational variability, the data are thereby explained (away).

12.2.3. Not Pre-Semantic

Whether an expression *e* gets employed and whether a sign *s* gets used in articulating *e* are contingent matters determined by speaker intentions and, perhaps, context. But how intentions (or context) determine whether it's *e* and *s* that a speaker is employing on a given occasion is *not* the same as how speaker intentions and contextual salience determine semantic values for context-sensitive expressions or conversational implicatures (or any other speech act exceeding semantic content). Nor is it pre-semantic in Kaplan's sense. Kaplan (1989: 559) says, 'Given an utterance, semantics cannot tell us what expression was uttered or what language it was uttered in. This is a pre-semantic task.' Similarly, if a word is ambiguous, semantics won't say which meaning is intended in a particular utterance. The effect a pre-semantic process has on semantic content is 'indirect'. Even though language selection influences the semantic content of the utterance, it does so indirectly through the determination of the input to the semantic machinery that

---

[4] Once signs are recognized as quotable items it should be obvious that there will be expressions, namely, quotation expressions, that can be articulated in one medium but not in others—a case of the tail wagging the dog.

churns out semantic content. And the choice we must make when confronted with ambiguity has the same pre-semantic, hence 'indirect', effect on semantic content.

In this regard, a speaker's choice of a sign system is *not* even pre-semantic. *After* disambiguation and language selection have occurred, a choice still remains of which sign system to exploit on an occasion of articulation, but this choice has no impact—direct or indirect—on semantic content. For suppose P is a proposition A wants to express in a language L with a sentence S. He can articulate S only after choosing a sign T. However, T must articulate S in order to express P or else A has made a mistake. Of course, an element of context sensitivity remains (though not semantic): which sign is used on a given occasion is itself determined in context. But this is true no matter how you twist and turn the data, so it should come as no surprise.

These claims are a good first (and independently motivated) effort at explaining (away) the recalcitrant variability data. They obviously require further development—more than we can hope for here, but we can go further; for we can explain *why* theorists (including former time-slices of ourselves) and informants have missed this explanation of the data, i.e. we can answer (Q2). In the next section, we propose three such explanations.

12.3. WHY THEORISTS AND INFORMANTS FAIL

There are many reasons why theorists and informants fail to distinguish sentences with distinct quotation expressions (i.e. why they're blind to the nature of quotable items). There are various hurdles an interpreter must get over in order to identify correctly a particular quotation expression. We'll survey some in what follows (though we don't intend this discussion to be exhaustive). Failure to get over any one of these can easily lead to a misidentification of a quotation expression, and so of what it quotes.

12.3.1. From Tokens to Signs

Each interpreter begins with a physical token. His first task is to figure out which sign this physical token instantiates. This problem does not admit of an easy solution.

First of all, two tokens might be physically indistinguishable and yet still constitute distinct signs. A sign is the sign it is not merely because of intrinsic physical properties but also by virtue of its relationship to other signs in a sign system. In effect, sign systems are sets or bundles of contrastive properties where each member of a sign system differs from every other member at least with respect to one of these properties. This, of course, is compatible with two tokened signs from different sign systems being physically indistinguishable.

Secondly, in the other direction, physically distinguishable items might be the same sign. Suppose two speakers send emails to each other using figures of different sizes. These physical differences might not matter for the purposes of exchange, and so, may not suffice for distinguishing signs. In this regard, with respect to some sign system, an 'a' and an 'a' may be the same sign—though physically distinct. Size doesn't always matter.

As we already noted, to determine which sentence is being articulated on a given occasion, a speaker must first determine whether physically distinct symbols flanking a tokened identity sign are the same signs or not.

This shouldn't be too surprising; after all, no two handwritings are identical. People make a career out of being able to pin a person to a scrawl. Yet no one wants to infer that the signs employed in any two distinguishable handwritings are distinct. The output of pencils, pens, chalk, keyboards, and other sign-producing devices might be physically distinct without their signs being so.

A second problem we encounter in deciphering another's message arises inasmuch as quotation expressions can quote (at least) signs and expressions.

12.3.2. From Signs to Expressions

The problem broached in the previous section concerns the individuation of signs—a topic the details of which are better left to non-philosophers, but whose basic structure should be easy enough to grasp. We hope simply to have said enough to show why we might misidentify a quotation expression when confronted with its token. Notice that since expressions are once removed from the signs that articulate them, when a quoted item is an expression and not a sign, the problem of quotation expression identification is only compounded.

For even after correctly identifying the signs in play with regards to any articulated quotation sentence, we still must ascertain whether its quoted item is the sign used in articulating the quotation expression or the expression that that sign articulates (if any).

Once again, returning to García-Carpintero's description of the data, we are asked to imagine a true utterance of (7.6.1). Our preferred way of couching the request is, having identified the sign or signs used in articulating two quotation expressions flanking an identity, we next need to determine which expressions they articulate. One sign might articulate a quotation expression that contains a sign as its constituent and another might articulate a quotation expression that contains an expression, say, the name for the capital of Spain, as its constituent. We then have a false statement. If they both articulate quotation expressions that contain expressions, then we have a true statement.[5]

Note that if the quotation expressions that identical signs articulate have distinct semantic values, it follows directly from our syntactic account that the expressions themselves are distinct (because their constituents — their semantic values — are distinct). So, even having identified the signs employed on a given occasion, we still have our work cut out for us. We still need to determine which expressions are being articulated. This extra work provides us with yet another opportunity for failure.

12.3.3. Quotation Across Sign Systems

Once you recognize differences between signs and the physical types their tokens instantiate, and also between expressions and the signs used in articulating them, some of the confusion surrounding the recalcitrant data becomes transparent. Since we can articulate the same expression in indefinitely many sign systems, we can quote the same expression in indefinitely many sign systems. But we *can't* quote the same sign in indefinitely many sign systems. Indeed, it's unclear whether a sign from one sign system can be quoted in any other sign system.

---

[5] There is another issue of whether we say of a single sign that it articulates expressions that differ in meaning — i.e. whether the expressions are the same and just the meanings differ. Does 'color' pick out one expression that is both a noun and a verb or are two distinct expressions articulated by a single sign? What about 'bank' — can it pick out a single expression with two meanings — or is a single sign used to articulate distinct words with two meanings? Once the distinction between signs and expressions is on the table we have another dimension with which to describe lots of potentially puzzling data. Note, however, that with quotational expressions this maneuver is unavailable, for reasons given in the text.

According to the strong disquotational principle, whatever is quoted must be contained in the quotation expression that quotes it. So if a sign is quoted by a quotation expression, then that sign must be contained in that quotation expression. We also assumed earlier that what individuates signs are certain contrastive features. If these differ between sign systems T1 and T2, then no sign from T1 can be quoted in T2.[6] To that extent, sign quotation is sign system bound.[7]

12.3.4. Summary of Answer to Q2

Differences can result when distinct signs are exploited and/or invoked. However we conceive of sign individuation, it is not the same as ambiguity or semantic-context sensitivity, that is, differences in meaning are not driving this discussion. In the different cases described, the same quotation expression is not employed throughout. Rather, in the recalcitrant cases, distinct quotation expressions discuss different quotable items. Differences in the signs used are (partly) responsible. Differences in intuited truth-value do not reflect semantic-context sensitivity, then, since no expression has its semantic value determined by its context of utterance. Differences in sentential truth-value are due to differences in sentences (and thus expressions) articulated.

12.4. CONCLUSION

Where have we gotten to? Different information might be conveyed by the same expressions on distinct occasions of use, and so we understand

---

[6] We don't mean to say that this follows logically from anything established above. It does seem to be a piece of data that if two quotation expressions contain different signs, they can't be the same quotation expression, but we don't know a proof that this must be so.

[7] Why assume that nothing more basic than signs and expressions can be quoted? If there are true sentences of the form '' . . . ' is not a sign in any sign system or an expression in any language' (where some quotable item replaces the three dots), then there must be quotable items that exist outside sign systems and languages. It may be that non-philosophical use of quotation supports the hypothesis that there are such items (we consider that question up for further investigation). What is crucial is that if the class of quotable items turns out to contain entities other than signs and expressions, the structure of the view defended in this chapter is preserved. According to the containment invoked in QS, any quotable item must enter into the individuation conditions for quotation expressions in the same way that signs and expressions do. That's the principle invoked by our explanation of the recalcitrant data. So we wouldn't be too bothered were it to turn out that the metaphysics of quotable items incorporates more than signs and expressions.

why someone might mistakenly conclude that a given expression is semantically context-sensitive when it is not. However, as we argued in Ch. 7, quotation is not semantically context-sensitive. For one, if it were, we would be forced to relinquish something sacred about quotation—namely, its disquotational nature. A consequence of accepting the Minimal Theory from Ch. 11 is the surprising result that quotation expressions contain their semantic values as constituents. Once embraced, a strategy for explaining the appearance of context sensitivity for quotation that goes beyond the scope of standard pragmatic explanations can be exploited in explaining some variability data. Key to the solution is to see that quotation expressions can quote not only expressions but also signs. That distinction, as we have made clear, is well evidenced independently of any considerations about the theory of quotation. We ended with a series of explanations for why theorists have failed to recognize that physically indistinguishable tokens might yield distinct quotation expressions.

The theory of quotation—the Minimal Theory—that we have worked our way up to in this book—compounded with the theory of quotation expression individuation endorsed in this chapter—provide, we believe, a rather elegant story about the nature of quotation, but much work remains.

As we see it, a number of important questions require further investigation, some of which are:

- What are signs and how are they individuated?
- What are expressions and how are they individuated?
- What is it to know an expression or a sign?
- And do signs and expressions exhaust the set of quotable items?

As we pointed out, we predict that answers to these questions do not depend on any particularly important philosophical concern. These are largely empirical issues, better left to non-philosophers. But any answer to these questions will preserve the structure of the solution presented here, as long as the notion of containment in QS is preserved. In that sense, the complete theory of quotation of this book is amenable to a rather wide range of implementations.

References

Atlas, J. 1989. *Philosophy without Ambiguity* (Oxford: Oxford University Press).

Benbaji, Y. 2004*a*. 'A Demonstrative Analysis of 'Open Quotation''. *Mind and Language* 19/5: 534–47.

—— 2004b. 'Using Others' Words'. *Journal of Philosophical Research* 29: 93–112.

—— 2005. 'Who Needs Semantics of Quotation Marks?' *Belgian Journal of Linguistics Yearbook*, 27–49.

Bennett, J. 1988. 'Quotation'. *Noûs* 22: 399–418.

Burge, T. 1986. ''On Davidson's 'Saying that'''', in E. Lepore (ed.), *Truth and Interpretation*. (Oxford: Basil Blackwell), 190–208.

Cappelen, H. 1999. 'Intentions in Words'. *Noûs*, 33 1: 92–102.

—— and Dever, J. 2001. 'Believing in Words'. *Synthese* 127: 279–301.

—— and Lepore, E. 1997*a*. 'On an Alleged Connection between Semantic Theory and Indirect Quotation'. *Mind and Language* 12: 278–96.

—— 1997*b*. 'Varieties of Quotation'. *Mind* 106: 429–50.

—— 1998. 'Using, Mentioning, and Quoting: Reply to Tsohatzidis'. *Mind* 107: 665–6.

—— 1999*a*. 'Reply to Pietroski', in Murasugi and Stainton, 283–5.

—— 1999*b*. 'Semantics of Quotation', in Zeglen, 90–9.

—— 2004. *Insensitive Semantics* (Oxford: Basil Blackwell).

—— 2005. 'Varieties of Quotation Revisited'. *Belgian Journal of Linguistics Yearbook*, 51–75.

—— 2006. 'Reply to Hawthorne'. *Philosophy and Phenomenological Research*, 473–80.

Carnap, R. 1947. *Meaning and Necessity* (Chicago: University of Chicago Press).

Chomsky, N. 1959. 'On Certain Formal Properties of Grammars'. *Information and Control* 2: 137–67.

—— 2000. *New Horizons in the Study of Language and Mind* (Cambridge: Cambridge University Press).

Christensen, N. 1967. 'The Alleged Distinction between Use and Mention'. *Philosophical Review* 76: 358–67.

Clark, H. H. 1996. *Using Language* (Cambridge: Cambridge University Press).

—— and Gerrig, R. 1990. 'Quotations as Demonstrations'. *Language* 66 4: 764–805.

CRAM, D. F. 1978. 'The Syntax of Direct Quotation'. *Cahiers de Lexicologie* 33: 41–52.

CRESSWELL, M., and VON STECHOW, A. 1982. 'De Re Belief Generalized'. *Linguistics and Philosophy* 5: 503–35.

CUMMING, S. 2005. 'Dynamic Quotation'. *Belgian Journal of Linguistics* 17: 77–88.

DAVIDSON, D. 1968. 'On Saying That', repr. in *Inquiries Into Truth and Interpretation*, 2nd edn. (Oxford: Oxford University Press, 2001), ii. 93–108.

—— 1979. 'Quotation', ibid. 79–92. Originally published in *Theory and Decision* 11: 27–40.

—— 1999. 'Reply to Cappelen and Lepore', in Zeglen, 100–2.

ELUGARDO, R. 1999. 'Mixed Quotation', in Murasugi and Stainton, 223–44.

FREGE, G. 1892. 'On Sense and Reference', repr. in P. Geach and M. Black (eds.), *Translations from the Philosophical Writings of Gottlob Frege*, 3rd edn. (Oxford: Basil Blackwell, 1980), 56–78.

GARCÍA-CARPINTERO, M. 1994. 'Ostensive Signs: Against the Identity Theory of Quotation'. *Journal of Philosophy* 91: 253–64.

—— 2004. 'The Deferred Ostension Theory of Quotation'. *Noûs* 38 4: 674–92.

—— 2005. 'Double Duty Quotation: The Deferred Ostension Account', *Belgian Journal of Linguistics Yearbook*, 89–108.

GEACH, P. 1957. *Mental Acts* (London: Routledge & Kegan Paul).

GODDARD, L., and ROUTLEY, R. 1966. 'Use, Mention, and Quotation'. *Australasian Journal of Philosophy* 44: 1–49.

GOLDSTEIN, L. 1984. 'Quotation of Types and Types of Quotation'. *Analysis* 44: 1–6.

GOMEZ-TORRENTE, M. 2001. 'Quotation Revisited'. *Philosophical Studies* 102: 23–53.

—— 2005. 'Remarks on Impure Quotation', *Belgian Journal of Linguistics Yearbook*, 129–52.

GRICE, H. P. 1989. *Studies in the Way of Words* (Cambridge, Mass.: Harvard University Press).

JORGENSEN, JULIA, MILLER, GEORGE, and SPERBER, DAN. 1984. 'Test of the Mention Theory of Irony'. *Journal of Experimental Psychology: General* 113: 112–20.

KAPLAN, D. 1989. 'Demonstratives', in J Almog, J. Perry, and H. Wettstein (eds.), *Themes from Kaplan* (Oxford: Oxford University Press) 481–564.

—— 1990. 'Words'. *Aristotelian Society*, suppl. vol. 64: 93–119.

KRIPKE, S. 1977. 'Speaker's Reference and Semantic Reference'. *Midwest Studies in Philosophy* 2: 255–76.

LARSON, R. K., and Ludlow, P. 1993. 'Interpreted Logical Forms'. *Synthese* 95: 305–55.

LEPORE, E. 1999. 'The Scope and Limits of Quotation', in L. Hahn (ed.), *The Philosophy of Donald Davidson* (New York: Open Court), 691–714.

LINSKY, L. 1950. 'On Using Inverted Commas'. *Methodos* 2: 232–6.

LUDWIG, K., and Ray, G. 1998. 'Semantics for Opaque Contexts'. *Philosophical Perspectives* 12: 141–66.

MALCOLM, J. 1990. *The Journalist and the Murderer.* (New York: Random House).

MATES, B. 1972. *Elementary Logic*, 2nd edn. (Oxford: Oxford University Press).

MUNRO, P. 1982. 'On the Transitivity of Say-Verbs', in P. Hopper and S. Thompson (eds.), *Studies in Transitivity: Syntax and Semantics* (New York: Academic Press), 301–18.

MURASUGI, K., and STAINTON, R. (eds.) 1999. *Philosophy and Linguistics* (Boulder Colo.: Westview).

NEALE, S. 1993. 'Term Limits'. *Philosophical Perspectives* 7: 89–124.

_____ 2000. 'On Being Explicit: Comments on Stanley and Szabo, and on Bach'. *Mind and Language* 15: 284–94.

PARSONS, T. 1982. 'What Do Quotation Marks Name? Frege's Theories of Quotations and That-clauses'. *Philosophical Studies* 42: 315–28.

PARTEE, B. 1973. 'The Syntax and Semantics of Quotation', in S. R. Anderson and P. Kiparsky (eds.), *A Festschrift for Morris Halle* (New York: Holt, Rinehart & Winston), 410–18.

POSTAL, P. 2004. *Skeptical Linguistic Essays* (Oxford: Oxford University Press).

PREDELLI, S. 2003. 'Scare Quotes and their Relation to Other Semantic Issues'. *Linguistics and Philosophy* 26 1: 1–28.

_____ 2005. ' 'Subliminable' Messages, Scare Quotes, and the Use Hypothesis'. *Belgian Journal of Linguistics Yearbook*, 153–66.

PRIOR, A. 1971. *Objects of Thought* (Oxford: Oxford University Press).

QUINE, W. V. O. 1940. *Mathematical Logic* (Boston, Mass.: Harvard University Press).

_____ 1959. *Methods of Logic* (New York: Henry Holt).

_____ 1960. *Word and Object* (Cambridge, Mass.: MIT).

_____ 1961*a*. *From a Logical Point Of View* (Cambridge, Mass.: Harvard University Press).

_____ 1961*b*. 'Reference and Modality', in 1961*a*, 139–59.

_____ 1966. 'Three Grades of Modal Involvement', in *The Ways of Paradox* (New York: Random House), 156–74.

_____ 1970. *Philosophical Logic* (New York: Prentice Hall).

RAMSEY, F. P. (1927). 'Facts and Propositions', *Aristotelian Society*, suppl. vol. 7: 153–70

RECANATI, F. 2000. *Oratio Obliqua, Oratio Recta: An Essay on Metarepresentation* (Cambridge, Mass.: MIT).

_____ 2001. 'Open Quotation'. *Mind* 110: 637–87.

REICHENBACH, H. 1947. *Elements of Symbolic Logic* (New York: Free Press).

REIMER, M. 1996. 'Quotation Marks: Demonstratives or Demonstrations?' *Analysis* 56: 131–42.

_____ 2005. 'Too Counter-Intuitive to Believe? Pragmatic Accounts of Mixed Quotation'. *Belgian Journal of Linguistics Yearbook*, 167–86.

RICHARD, M. 1986. 'Quotation, Grammar, and Opacity'. *Linguistics and Philosophy* 9: 383–403.

_____ 2005. 'Did I Mention What He Said?' unpublished MS.

SAKA, P. 1998. 'Quotation and the Use-Mention Distinction'. *Mind* 107: 113–35.

_____ 1999. 'Quotation: A Reply to Cappelen & Lepore'. *Mind* 108 432: 751–4.

_____ 2005. 'Quotation Constructions'. *Belgian Journal of Linguistics Yearbook*, 87–112.

SALMON, N. 1986. *Frege's Puzzle* (Cambridge, Mass: MIT).

SCHLENKER, P. 2003. 'A Plea for Monsters'. *Linguistics & Philosophy* 26: 29–120.

SEARLE, J. 1969. *Speech Acts* (Cambridge: Cambridge University Press), 4.1.

SELLARS, W. 1954. 'Presupposing'. *Philosophical Review* 63: 197–215.

SEYMOUR, D. 1996. 'Content and Quotation'. *Rivista di Linguistica* 8/2: 309–29.

SIMCHEN, O. 1999. 'Quotational Mixing of Use and Mention'. *The Philosophical Quarterly* 49/196: 325–36.

SMULLYAN, R. M. 1957. 'Languages in which Self Reference is Possible'. *Journal of Symbolic Logic* 22: 55–67.

SOAMES, S. 1989. 'Semantics and Semantic Competence'. *Philosophical Perspectives*, 575–96.

_____ 2002. *Beyond Rigidity; The Unfinished Agenda of Naming and Necessity* (Oxford: Oxford University Press).

_____ 2005. 'Naming and Asserting', in Z. Szabo (ed.), *Semantics vs. Pragmatics* (Oxford: Oxford University Press), 256–82.

STAINTON, R. 1999. 'Remarks on the Syntax and Semantics of Mixed Quotation', in Murasugi and Stainton, 259–78.

SZABO, Z. 2006. 'Sensitivity Training'. *Mind and Language*. 21: 31–8.

TARSKI, A. 1933. 'The Concept of Truth in Formalized Languages', repr. in Tarski, *Logic, Semantics, Metamathematics*, 2nd edn. (Indianapolis: Hackett, 1983), 152–278.

TSOHATZIDIS, S. 1998. 'The Hybrid Theory of Mixed Quotation'. *Mind* 107: 661–4.

_____ 2005. 'Lost Hopes and Mixed Quotes'. *Belgian Journal of Linguistics Yearbook*, 213–29.

WALLACE, J. 1972. 'On the Frame of Reference', in D. Davidson and G. Harman (eds.), *Semantics of Natural Language* (Dordrecht: Reidel), 219–52.

WASHINGTON, C. 1992. 'The Identity Theory of Quotation'. *Journal of Philosophy* 89: 582–605.

WERTHEIMER, R. 1999. 'Quotation Apposition'. *Philosophical Quarterly* 49/197: 514–19.

ZEGLEN, U. 1999. *Donald Davidson: Truth, Meaning and Knowledge* (London: Routledge).

Index